THE WOMEN'S CIRCLE

Hardie Grant

BOOKS

THE WOMEN'S CIRCLE

ANOUSHKA FLORENCE

I

WOMEN'S CIRCLES 12

WHAT IS A WOMEN'S CIRCLE? 15

II

PLANNING YOUR CIRCLE 26

PREPARING THE CIRCLE 28
CREATING THE SPACE 40
THE CIRCLE 48

III

HOLDING YOUR CIRCLE 60

NATURE 62
The Moon 65   The Sun 81   Seasons 119

NURTURE 136
New Beginnings 139   Honouring Endings 145   Manifestation 159

RITES OF PASSAGE 164
Maiden 167   Mama 181   Crone 195

Closing Words 206   Acknowledgements 206

FOREWORD

EVER SINCE I WAS A LITTLE GIRL,
I FELT THE CALLING OF THE CIRCLE.

I was drawn towards the ritual of gathering, the coming together of friends and family, and the safety I felt when contained in it all.

Growing up in a tight-knit Jewish community, I witnessed the coming together of people who gathered to mark holy days, new moons, seasonal festivals, coming of ages and transitions of both love and loss.

These markers rooted in me a deep knowing of how much we all need one another. The longing to gather, to be seen and to be witnessed holds the key to so much of what I believe we all collectively seek. As I learnt very early on, we were not meant to do life alone.

That experience was paired with a bohemian mama who create sacred spaces for a living. As a little girl I used to watch as she transformed people's homes into havens. Our house was constantly changing, dependent on her mood. Furniture would move around, walls would change colour, smells would waft.

She showed me the importance of spaces, and their power to hold and move energy. She passed this gift down to me, a gift that was passed down to her by her mother, and her mother and her mother – the red thread that had always known the importance of sacred spaces.

As I grew, I found myself stepping away from more organised patriarchal religion as I sought out a path of my own. I yearned to find a deeper connection to myself, to understand my feminine nature, to move through the cycles of Womanhood in a more holistic way. I needed to figure out who I was and what I truly wanted

from life. I believe that at some point in our lives, we are all called to leave what we know, in search of a deeper journey that calls us.

As I navigated my own way through the quest and all the challenges that life presents, I found myself calling out for a place where I could take refuge and find solace. A space to be seen, to be heard, to be witnessed. A space to re-centre as I journeyed deeper and deeper on my path. A space to gather with others, to belong and to remember that although this was my path to take, I didn't have to do it alone.

Ah, the Circle, it was calling me again.

And so, not knowing where to find spaces like this, I decided to create them for myself. As I sought other Women who wanted to gather in a space like this, I realised this longing was based on a thread so much deeper than I could ever imagine; a thread that I now know is woven into every Woman: the thread of the Women's Circle.

The intention of this book is to reconnect us all back to the threads within us, the threads that unify us, that weave us together.

I believe this book is needed now, more than ever. Having been separated from one another for so long, my wish is that as we do return to gathering, we do so with meaning, with intention, with sacredness.

As such, this book is an ode to reviving the ancient feminine practice of the Women's Circle with the intention of bringing meaning, symbolism and healing back to the moments in our lives when we need them most.

7

WHO IS THIS BOOK FOR?

This book is for any Woman hearing the calling to hold or be held in a Circle.

I use the terms Woman/Women/her/she throughout the book, but I want to make it clear that this extends to all female-identifying and non-binary beings. Your magik is recognised and your power is known.

For the sake of simplicity, this book has been written through the lens of the Woman holding the Circle. One Woman is typically the space holder in a Circle; her responsibility is to prepare, create and hold the space as outlined in this book. Of course, the space holder participates in the Circle as well – however, she will have more to do, so keep that in mind, and take it in turns to hold Circles for each other.

Please remember, the nature of the Circle means there is no hierarchy. Once in the Circle you will soon see how you each bring a different thread to the space, a thread of equal power and importance. These threads create the tapestry of the Circle.

HOW THIS BOOK WORKS

There is a certain flow to a Women's Circle – where beginning meets end, and end meets beginning. Generally, the flow of a Women's Circle will guide you to go on a journey, spiralling deeper and deeper into it until something within you shifts, and you are ready to re-emerge on the other side.

For the sake of this book, and with the intention to make these spaces accessible and easy for you to hold on your own, I have created a general Circle template that you can weave into any of the Circles described in this book.

Throughout this book you will find a beautiful array of Circles you can hold to serve you at different times and moments in your life. Each will follow the format opposite, but will explore different rituals, practices and ideas to weave in.

Once you become familiar with the flow, your Circle will become a safe vessel that the magik will just flow through. The journey starts here, so let's begin.

WOMEN'S CIRCLE MANDALA

PREPARE + SET UP ALTARSCAPES

OPEN SPACE

ENERGY TALK

MEDITATION

SHARING PROMPTS

CARD PULLING

RITUAL

CLOSING SPACE

WOMEN'S CIRCLES

*   *   *

WHAT IS A WOMEN'S CIRCLE?

A WOMEN'S CIRCLE IS A SACRED SPACE CREATED INTENTIONALLY FOR WOMEN TO GATHER.

It is a space where Women come together and sit in a sacred Circle created with the intention of making Women feel seen, safe, heard, held and witnessed on their journeys through life.

A sacred space free of judgement, competition, expectation, pressure or noise. A sacred space void of the demands from the outside world, a space just for us, to go inwards, to reconnect, to return home. A refuge for the spirit of the feminine.

All over the world, Women are returning, gathering under the moon in a small city apartment, bathing together in wild streams, holding ceremonies under ancient trees, creating sacred spaces in local parks, yoga centres, living rooms, backyards.

All over the world, Women are remembering how to hold space for each other. All over the world, Women are beginning to gather in this way. If you are hearing the call, then you are being called to gather too.

How do you know if you're ready to hold one?

Well, the calling is the initiation. If you are holding this book in the palms of your hands, no matter how it arrived there, this is the very sign you need to know that the Circle is calling you.

So listen, pay attention to the longing within, trust where you are being led, and remember, the Circle lives within each of us.

You already have everything you need in order to begin.

I know many of you may be wondering, *'How will I know what to do? Where do I even begin?'*

Ah, my darling, there is so much to share ... so let's start from the very beginning.

WOMEN'S CIRCLES ARE ANCIENT,
DEEP WITHIN US WE KNOW THEM,
WE FEEL THEM, WE LONG FOR THEM.

WHEN WE STEP BACK INTO THEM,
WE FEEL THE WOMEN BEFORE US,
THE ONES WHO KNEW THEIR DIVINITY,
THE ONES WHO WERE FREE.

YET WITH THAT,
WE ALSO FEEL THE PAIN,
THE PAIN OF THE SUPPRESSION
THAT BROKE THESE CIRCLES AWAY.

AND THUS EVERY TIME WE STEP BACK INTO CIRCLE,
WE ARE CALLING OUR POWER BACK,
THE LIGHT AND THE DARK, THE WISDOM AND THE MAGIK.

THROUGH A COLLECTIVE HEALING,
AND A COLLECTIVE REMEMBERING,
WE AWAKEN.

WE DO THIS FOR OUR GRANDMOTHERS.
WE DO THIS FOR OUR DAUGHTERS.
WE DO THIS FOR OUR SISTERS,
OUR MOTHERS, OURSELVES.

FOR THERE IS NO SAFER SPACE
FOR A WOMAN
THAN A SPACE HELD
BY THE SACREDNESS OF THE CIRCLE.

A SPACE FOR YOU TO REMEMBER, WHO YOU REALLY ARE.
AND IN REMEMBERING, WHO YOU REALLY ARE,
YOU LET GO OF WHO THEY TOLD YOU TO BE.

ORIGINS OF THE CIRCLE

A Circle with a sacred centre is the oldest known form of social interaction. This is how communities would have gathered to interact, eat, commune and pass down wisdom and stories. A place where all generations could come together to share in life.

As such, the remanence of the Circle can be found in every single ancient culture; the shape that has always created space for the whole to belong.

The Women's Circle can be seen to have emerged from this; a realisation of the need to separate the energy of the feminine and masculine in order for them to come into balance. With each energy holding its own unique power, it was important for the village as a whole to create the spaces in which they could retreat.

The first Circles that were documented span back to 800 CE, and stem from African roots. Typically, these were spaces created to support Women during the time of menstruation. Living in close proximity to one another, it wouldn't have been unusual for a whole village to be mensturating at the same time. For as some of you may have experienced in your own lives, our cycles tend to sync with women we live closely with. Women's Circles, Moon Lodges, Menstrual Huts, Red Tents are some of the names used to describe these sacred spaces created for Women.

Living in alignment with both nature, and the nature within them, their bleed was a marker to retreat. Women would leave their villages to commune in a hut all together, leaving their day-to-day lives, their families and their usual responsibilities behind. These spaces were created in order for Women to rest, to support one another and to be given the space to go inwards. For it was believed that Women were at their most powerful during this time.

Communities would ask Bleeding Women to use this time to ask the spirits for guidance and messages for the wider village. Women would receive and channel prophetic visions that they could relate to their communities once their cycles came to an end. There was a deep understanding of the connection Women had to nature and the power they held, especially at this time. As such, the Red Tent was a reverent space; a space of healing, of letting go, of dreaming up a new future.

The traditions of these spaces can be found throughout many different communities, villages and towns across the world. These spaces held such deep feminine needs that all over the world, Women would unite without even knowing it, in this sacred space.

However, a Women's Circle was not just reserved for honouring the time of a Woman's bleed. These spaces were community spaces, spaces where Women could gather and put the world to rights.

In some Native American tribes, they were places to discuss issues in the village, using the Circle as a safe space to hold different opinions and ideas. In Pakistan they are called Bashalis, a sacred space for women to gather, where men were strictly forbidden. These spaces created a sense of freedom, and liberation from women's responsibilities. Creating a breathing space for women to just be. In Pagan communities, they were often used to honour the moon cycles, the seasons and the solstices.

In Judaism, Women would gather on every New Moon to celebrate the beginning of a new cycle ahead.

Women's Circles are still being held in many First Nations communities around the world. Having heard the whispers that Women's Circles were still alive and communing in First Nations communities, I got in touch with a Woman running them in Australia. I asked her if she would be open to sharing any insight into the traditions and rituals that occur in these spaces.

Her response helped reinforce the significance of the Circle. She shared that this knowledge is sacred, and what happens in the Circle stays in the Circle. The truth is, it was hard to research the history of women's circles, but this is simply because these spaces are, and have always been, sacred. As the Woman in Australia relayed to me, what happens in the circle stays in the circle. We do not need to document these spaces to prove they exist, for they live within each of us.

We each hold a sacred thread that runs through our female lineage; a thread that, if we go deep enough, will lead us back to the time when our ancestors sat in a sacred Circle.

As such, the history lives on through us. My invitation is for you to find your thread.

I promise, the moment you step back into the Circle, you will begin to feel it, the remembering, the holding, the sacredness. The more you step into it, the deeper this memory will grow. And you will find your own history – or herstory, shall we say.

WHAT HAPPENED TO THE CIRCLES?

As we have seen, for some cultures, the Circles never disappeared. Cultures where nature remains at the centre held onto the importance of these sacred spaces for Women to gather. Yet for most of us in the Western world, as patriarchy and organised religion grew, feminine spaces, nature-based rituals, traditions and communities became forbidden – so much so that in the 15th century, *The Hammer of the Witches* publication was released. This was an in-depth guide stating how to hunt and persecute Women in their power. This marked the beginning of the destruction of feminine spiritual traditions and teachings.

This text would go on to inspire over 200 years of persecution of Women, leading into the witch trials. Women were burnt at the stake in a massacre that haunts us to this very day. Women who were once revered and honoured, were now feared and being hunted.

This marked the beginning of the end, for it wasn't safe for us to gather anymore, to hold these spaces, to connect and to share. Under the reign of the Patriarchy, anyone who held power was forced to surrender it. Men were threatened by the power Women held, and so Women were forced to hide it, to bury it. Most buried it so deeply that they forgot where it was hiding.

For hundreds of years, Women have denied themselves access to their power, access to the sacred spaces that hold their power, and the treasures that are found in the ancient practice of the Women's Circle.

Women all over the world are feeling the earth shake beneath them as the calling to return back to our power emerges. We are realising that we never forgot it, we just had to bury it deep inside us to protect ourselves, our sisters and our daughters. We had to hide it away, for that was the only way we could survive.

But my sisters, we are now standing on the edge of herstory, which is calling for us to return.

Women's Circles are popping up all over the world, like seeds that were planted many moons ago by the Women who came before us. Seeds of hope that we would one day remember our power, our magik and the Circles that hold us.

The time is now. We have been waiting hundreds of years for a time when we could feel safe to gather once more.

So perhaps it's your turn now. Deep within you, you are hearing the call of the Women who came before you, to unearth the wisdom of the Circle. Perhaps if you close your eyes now, and get really still ... you may even uncover the remembrance of a Circle within you that once was. So go on, close your eyes, take a deep breath. And perhaps you may see a Circle of Women gathering, around a fire. And perhaps you may begin to pay attention, to where you are, to who is there. And perhaps it is here you may realise, that it has always been inside of you. This book is an invitation to step back in, to rediscover the power that lives within you, the power you hold to release, to heal, to vision, to dream and to manifest a world for you and those around you. The power that lies in the Women's Circle. Are you ready to step back in?

MY JOURNEY TO THE CIRCLE

The Circles I hold have been inspired by the teachings I've received from wise Women who have come into my life, as well as by my own practices and the wisdom of my ancestors.

Inspired by my visions of how the Women who came before me would have gathered, I have sought to recreate the ancient mystic ways alluded to by Kabbalistic and Jewish texts. I envisioned my great, great, great grandmothers gathering in a Circle under the new moon crescent in a sacred tent somewhere far, far away.

Weaving together the ancient wisdom of my female line, who passed down the gift of creating sacred spaces, and the rich Kabalistic mysticism of my ancestors who knew the power of ritual.

Weaving together the journey I've been on as a spiritual seeker, learning from many beautiful traditions and cultures. Inspired by the Shamanic teachings, Pagan traditions and Eastern cultures, and all I've learnt from them.

Weaving in my own practice of prayer, meditation and my growing connection to nature.

My spaces are not just based on one thing, they are everything. They are all parts of me, they are the gifts I hold within. And as I hold my Circles, I become the vessel through which they can pass.

It is so important that when we create our Circles, you tune into the gifts, practices and ideas you have to offer. Seek not to take from other cultures, but rather trust what inspires you, what you've learnt, and what you authentically have to offer.

For example, I don't cast a Circle, I open a Circle. Casting a Circle belongs to the Pagan traditions, and while I admire and honour them, it's not part of my story. Rather, I get quiet with myself and ask to be guided to what feels authentic to me.

As you navigate your way through this book and create your own Circles, keep asking yourself what is authentic to you, what feels good to you. Take what feels good and leave the rest. This is how you can truly weave authenticity into your spaces and offer the medicine that you have to share.

As you will soon realise, you already hold so much of what your Circle needs.

25

II

PLANNING YOUR CIRCLE

*   *   *

PREPARING THE CIRCLE
CREATING THE SPACE
THE CIRCLE

PREPARING THE CIRCLE

THE MAGIK OF THE CIRCLE
LIES IN THE INTENTION,
SO WE NEED TO PREPARE AS MUCH
AS WE CAN FOR EACH CIRCLE TO START
ACTIVATING THE ENERGY.

THE TRUTH IS, the main work of the Circle happens in the preparation. Everything you do in the lead-up to creating your Women's Circle, every thought you have around it, every action you take towards it, every bit of effort you put into manifesting this space is used to weave together an energy so that the space can become truly sacred.

The preparation is the work. You are creating the space through which the magik, the healing, the wisdom and the power of the Circle can come through.

I like to leave at least one whole moon cycle to prepare before a Women's Circle. However, I do invite you to work with the timeframe you have. If you're feeling the calling to hold it sooner, trust your intuition. Remember, all is in divine timing.

In this chapter we will explore how to consciously prepare for your Circles, knowing that the work happens long before the Circle even begins.

FOUR WEEKS BEFORE

SET YOUR INTENTION

Your Circle must stand firmly on the earth of an intention. Without a solid reason behind why you are holding the Circle, the Circle cannot bloom.

Tune into why you want to hold your Circle, what you are seeking to receive from it, what you would like others to feel from it, and let the following chapters inspire you in deciding how to bring it into life.

Once you've connected to your intention, you hold the power to infuse it into every step you take on the journey to creating it. This, my sister, is the secret ingredient in creating the magik.

Just like a temple, when you step inside of your Circle you will know that everything has been placed, created and designed with an intention of devotion and worship. As such, you will feel this energy as soon as you step into the space.

Once your intention is set and infused through the preparation of the Circle, Women will only need to step inside the sacred space you've created in order to feel it.

And just like magik, half the work is done.

CHOOSE A DATE

It is time to choose a date consciously. So often in life we make decisions without realising that there could be a more intentional way of doing so, and that making decisions more consciously has the power to greatly impact the end result.

When selecting a date for your Circle, know that you can work with the universe to support you, as different times of the day, month and year hold different energies.

Depending on what your intention is behind the Circle, you can consciously select a date that supports that.

See the section on Nature (in part II, starting on page 62) to see how you can work with the Moon, the Sun and Stars in order to align your Circle with hers. For the heart of a Women's Circle loves nothing more than to dance with the cycles of the universe.

FINDING A VENUE

Once your date is set, it's now time to decide where you're going to hold your Circle.

The choice of space is very important. You want your Circle to feel like a safe and sacred space. A space where you won't be disturbed, a space that's easy for people to get to, a space that can hold you all.

When I first started holding gatherings, I used my living room. I was living alone in a small apartment in London. I decided to fill my flat with house plants and dream catchers, and on some nights I would cram as many as twenty Women together into a tight-knit Circle. We'd sit on the floor with a jumbled spread of eclectic cushions, turn off all the lights and burn hundreds of candles.

You want a space that will align with your Circle, but you don't need to spend ages looking for the perfect Pinterest space. You just need a container that will hold you ... remember, you will create the sacredness in it.

So make it easy for yourself – usually the perfect space is right on your doorstep.

Ideas for spaces include:

☾ your home
☾ a friend's home
☾ a safe space in nature
☾ empty café or shop

Please note, if you hold your Circle in nature, be mindful that outsiders have the right to be there. So try to find somewhere in nature that is quiet.

Wherever you are holding the Circle, ensure you won't be disturbed, and that you can have the space for at least one hour beforehand, to prepare.

STRUCTURE

Decide what you're going to do in your Circle. Take inspiration from the chapters ahead as you weave together your flow.

It's important to have a plan for your Circle. It calms the mind, taking you out of your head and into your heart.

However, there is a balance between having a plan that creates space for fluidity, and having a plan that is so specific that it leaves no room for magik. The art of the Women's Circle lies in the magik that happens within the empty spaces, the silence and the arms of the unknown.

So spend some time creating a rough plan. Carve out the journey you would like to take these Women on. Prepare in all the ways you need to. But, most importantly, trust that it will all flow and be exactly what it needs to be by the time you step into the space.

You can use the basic template on page 11, adding your notes to each part you are looking to infuse.

THREE WEEKS BEFORE

INVITATION

Connect to those you want to gather at your Circle. Who would feel right to be there?

This will change depending on what type of Circle you're holding; always remember to be intentional with the Women you call in.

Perhaps there are Women you feel would love to join this Circle, or perhaps you're holding this Circle for a friend, a bride-to-be or your mother. Perhaps you feel pulled to send an invitation out to your community, trusting that whoever hears the call will respond.

What I found on my journey was that there were so many Women seeking a sacred space to gather, but there was nowhere to go. By creating this space you are facilitating it for you, for them, for the whole, and there is true healing just in that. I like to send out the calling three weeks in advance so the date is reserved and the energy begins to activate.

Words have power, so when writing your invitation, remember this is the first thing you are sending out, and this will be the first thing they receive. You want to ensure it sets the tone and energy for the Circle.

What to include in the invitation:

☾ name of Circle
☾ date
☾ where
☾ what to bring (if anything)
☾ what to wear if there is a special dress code

Get creative – you can draw, paint, collage, write or create a poem for the invite, all to reflect the theme of the Circle.

You can post it on social media, send it to your group of girls, or even go old-school with a printable flyer for your local community. Whatever you do, ensure it is done with intention ... and the power of your words will spread.

32

TWO WEEKS BEFORE

VISUALISING THE SPACE

Once you have set the energy into motion by sending out your calling, and you know when, where and what you're going to do in your Circle, it's the perfect time to start visualising the space.

You will need to think about how you want your dream space to look. Spend some time envisioning how this space will serve the energy you are trying to create. You can put together a Pinterest board, or just dream it up into being.

☾ How do you want it to feel?
☾ Should it be dark or light?
☾ Are there any colours, textures or sounds you feel you should weave in?

For example, if you were to hold a spring equinox ceremony, then perhaps light and airy would come to mind. In contrast, if you were holding a winter solstice gathering, you may think cosy and warm, candle-lit.

Each section has suggestions on what you can weave into your space, so don't worry too much ... but it's important that you can see the Circle in your mind's eye before it's created. This is part of visioning the Circle into being.

33

WOMEN'S CIRCLE CHECKLIST

Once you've visualised how the Circle will look, it's time to plan how you're going to make it happen.

☾ What decorations might you need to create your space?
☾ Do you have enough cushions, mats and rugs to make the space cosy?
☾ What will you need to gather?
☾ What can you consciously source that you don't already have?

I separate my checklist into three main categories.

SACRED SPACE

This will include any cushions, rugs or blankets. If you need more, you can always invite the Women to bring a cushion or rug each.

This also includes any technology you might need, such as speakers or lights.

MY RITUAL BASKET

I like to gather my essential tools in what I call my ritual basket. My invitation would be to call in your own ritual basket, and intentionally select the objects and tools that you can weave into your sacred space.

Please note, throughout this book, wherever I use the term 'ritual basket', this refers to all the components listed below.

Ritual cloth

This can be any type of tablecloth, piece of lace or fabric that you have. I lay this down in the middle of the Circle, and use it as the intentional space on which to build my altar.

Cleansing tools

These are sacred herbs, resins or wood that have been used for hundreds of years. They evoke the Medicine Woman within us, who knows that nature holds so much healing for us. Weaving them into our spaces is a powerful way to remind us of our innate connection to nature. I use my cleansing tools in every gathering to cleanse the energetic space and to close the energetic space. Typically, one would use a smudge stick, Palo Santo, incense or a tree resin.

As much as possible, try to find a cleansing tool that is indigenous to your land. Buy responsibly from sustainable sources, or try to forage your own.

I now grow sage, rosemary and lavender in my garden and use them to create my own smudge sticks. This can be a beautiful way to not only preserve these medicinal plants but also to bring a deep connection and meaning to your homegrown tools.

Candles + matches

I like to keep a Mother candle in my basket. This is typically a pillar candle that I can bring to each gathering to hold all the other candles. I light this candle first, and then light any tea lights or smaller candles from it. I like to think of the Mother candle as the light that holds us, transforms us and contains us during our gatherings.

I also ensure I have smaller candles and tea lights to dot around the space, and a big pack of matches.

Crystals

Crystals are the allies I weave in from the earth itself. Crystals hold such a powerful energy and have the capacity to bring so much healing, magik and support into your Women's Circle. Gather the crystals that will aid and support the intention behind your Circle, for crystals have the power to hold, expand and amplify the essence of your space in their very vibration. I usually thread them within the flower circle (see page 47) to charge and transmit the intentions we're setting. Throughout this book I've given examples of different crystals to bring in, but please trust your instincts and let yourself be guided by any crystals seeking to join your Women's Circle.

MY SMUDGE STICK RECIPE

GATHER

☾ six sprigs of foraged herbs;
I grow rosemary, sage and lavender in my garden,
so typically use whichever one I'm called to,
or sometimes all three.
Other herbs that are good for smudging include:
cedar, pine, sweetgrass, eucalyptus, mugwort,
cinnamon sticks and bay leaves.

☾ natural twine

☾ scissors

METHOD

I

Gather your foraged herbs,
as if you were making a small bouquet of flowers.

II

Take the twine and tie the bundle in a tight knot at the
bottom of the stems. Wrap the twine around the stems,
working your way up the bundle until you reach the top,
and then continuing back down until you reach the base again.

III

Cut the remaining twine off.

IV

Hang the bundle upside down in a dark dry cupboard
for at least one week before using.

Oracle deck

An Oracle deck is a tool you can use to receive messages from the universe/the divine/the goddess. It's an ancient feminine practice that aids Women in supporting their more psychic gifts. I use my deck in pretty much every Circle, introducing the cards and empowering Women to become their own card readers as they draw a card, receiving powerful messages and deeper insights into themselves. A deck of Oracle cards is a staple in my ritual basket.

I have always worked with Goddess cards, and have brought the same deck to every Circle I have held for the past six years. I like to stick to one deck, as I feel the power increases every time I use them. You may wish to go to a magikal shop, or type in 'Oracle decks' on Google and browse the Oracle card section. Ask to be guided to the perfect deck for you, and just trust what you're drawn to.

Please note, there are many different types of Oracle cards available, from Angel cards to spirit animal decks, Goddess cards to Affirmation cards. All these cards hold a slightly different energy, and vibration.

Don't worry if you've never worked with the cards before, they all come with a guide book that will enhance and support your relationship with them. The most important thing is to start your journey with intention, so trust what deck you're guided to, and begin there.

Pens + paper

In most Circles, there will be moments in the space where we will go into reflection and contemplation. This means it's super important to have enough paper and pens for the Circle. Messages, wisdom and insights will pour through the space, so making sure there is a physical space for these to be channelled is really supportive.

SPECIFIC CIRCLE INGREDIENTS

These are the items that are specific to the Circle you're holding. These will change for each gathering you hold; each Circle will have its own unique ingredients for the ritual and the altar space.

Spend the next few weeks sourcing, foraging and gathering anything you need to weave into the Circle. I've given you an ingredients list for every Circle described in this book, but feel free to gather anything else that holds meaning and calls you.

Add all the ingredients to your basket to brew and infuse in the lead-up to the Circle, knowing that there they are charging and sealing in the intention of the space.

A FEW DAYS BEFORE

WHAT TO WEAR

The ritual of getting dressed is such a deeply feminine practice, as what we wear does truly become an expression of our inner selves and our intentions. Whether you have chosen a dress code for your Circle or not, tune into what you want to wear, what colour may express the energy of the Circle and, most importantly, what makes you feel beautiful. Choose your garments in advance, and lay them out in the lead-up to the Circle.

MUSIC

The last step is to ensure that you have prepared a playlist, if you are thinking of playing music at your Circle. I like to begin my Circles with music, setting the tone energetically and vibrationally as the Women enter my space. I like to close my Circle with a song too, so they leave on the wings of music.

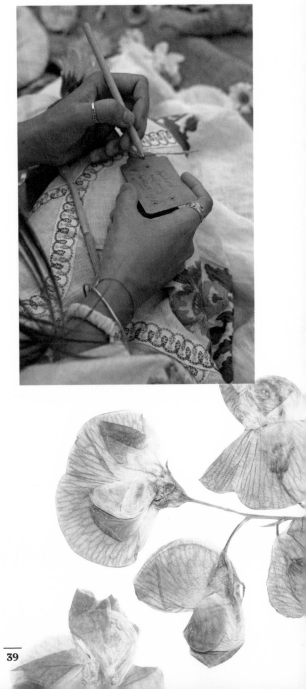

You may choose to play music at the beginning, the end, during or not at all; but if you do choose to play music, ensure you create a playlist that mirrors the energy you're seeking to create, and have it ready.

By this stage, you have prepared all that you can. You have set the energy into motion, and as I've said before, this will create the most powerful foundation, in which your Circle will bloom.

Where your attention goes, energy flows, so let's now flow into the day of the Circle and how you will create the space with that same awareness, presence and intention.

CREATING THE SPACE

SO IT'S THE day of your Circle. Everything has been prepared in advance, so there shouldn't be much left to do other than to create a space from your heart.

In preparing with intention, the energy has been set into motion. The universe is with you, so you can arrive into the day knowing that you are held, safe and supported, and that you have already created the most sacred container through which the Circle will flow.

CONFIRM DETAILS WITH YOUR TRIBE

Send a reminder to all the Women gathering to confirm the time, location and what they may need to bring with them. This will ensure the ease of the gathering as it unfolds.

It is also important to state that the gathering should begin punctually, and to explain the necessity of being on time. It is said that once a Circle opens, the energy has sealed in, so if people are late, they will break the circuit of energy when they step in.

GATHER YOUR SACRED SPACE ESSENTIALS AND YOUR RITUAL BASKET

Go through your Women's Circle checklist, and gather your ritual basket and all that you need. If you are making food, ensure you prepare as much as possible during the day, so you don't need to spend time cooking at the Circle.

CREATE YOUR SACRED SPACE

Head over to the location you are gathering at least one to two hours before the Circle begins. This will give you plenty of time to get ready, tune in and set up the space. It may also be necessary to clean the physical and energetic field of the space.

If you are in your home, your own personal energy will be dominating the space, and if you're in someone else's space, their energy will be dominating. Spend some time doing an energetic cleanse so the space is cleansed, neutral and pure. I like to do a broom purification.

Broom purification

Grab a broom and stand in the middle of the space. As you hold the broom, take three deep breaths, then begin to sweep from right to left. Walk counterclockwise as you spiral across the floor, visualising any energy being swept away with every motion.

You can bring a prayer in as you sweep, such as:

'Let anything that is not mine, let anything that is no longer serving me, be gone, now.'

Once you have swept the space, you may feel called to open some windows to welcome in fresh air, or to light some beautiful incense and invoke the energy with your intention for the Circle.

CREATING THE CIRCLE

Now that the space is cleared, it's time to weave your vision of the Circle into the space; to sprinkle the dream of what you envision this space being. Begin by creating your Circle using your sacred space essentials: the cushions, rugs and pillows you gathered. Place each down with the intention of creating a sacred space for each Woman to step into, as if you're blessing the space for each Woman before they even arrive.

Next, gather your ritual basket and step into the centre of the Circle. Perhaps take a moment here to close your eyes as you prepare to create your altar space. Remember, this is all a meditation, this is all sacred, this is all a part of the Circle itself.

Lay your ritual cloth down first, ensuring it sits in the centre of the Circle, then begin to place each object, tool and aspect of the altar down with intention.

You may feel called to create a mandala of sorts, using flowers – this is typically called a flower circle. This helps me to quiet my mind by using my hands, to get into my heart and adorn the Circle with intention. You will see in the chapters to come that I always include a flower circle.

DECORATING THE REST OF THE SPACE

Once your altar is created, ensure that the rest of the space looks how you wish it to. Lay out candles on surfaces or tables, prep any incense, and ensure you've connected your music to a speaker as you finish any last details.

GETTING READY

The Circle is set, the space has been created. Now it's time to fall deeper into the zone.

Getting ready for the Circle is a ritual, for you are getting dressed to sit in the temple you have built.

This can be a beautiful time to play some sensual music, put on some make-up, brush your hair, spray your favourite perfume and adorn yourself like a goddess. This is all a part of stepping back into your feminine power, welcoming your feminine energy in as you make yourself feel beautiful for the sacred space you are about to enter.

CENTRING

Once you finish getting ready, the Circle will begin to call you.

With probably only a few minutes to go before the Women begin to gather, this is your final moment to create your space, to light your candles, to play your playlist, to sit inside the Circle you have created, closing your eyes and whispering any wishes you have for the Circle into it.

Acknowledge yourself for all that you have done, and allow yourself to fall into the hands of the universe.

This is a moment to surrender, to trust that the Circle will guide you and support you, to know that all that is meant for the Circle already is, and all that is left is to simply let go.

FLOWER CIRCLE

I

Gather, forage or buy a bunch of flowers.
What kind will depend on the type of Circle you're holding,
but most importantly, be led by your intuition.

II

Once you've gathered your bunch,
set your intention for the Circle by holding the flowers
in the palms of your hands and blowing your wish onto them.

III

Begin by creating a small circle using the petals
or flower heads of your bunch of flowers.

IIII

Working from inside out, allow each flower circle
to get slightly bigger with every circle you make.

V

Keep going until you feel the circle is big enough.

VI

Get creative, let your heart lead, quiet the mind,
and infuse your flower circle with the intention of your space.

VII

Once you've created the flower circle, you can dot little
tea lights in between the circles, and add any of your ritual tools
into the circle also. Alternatively, you could just place your
ritual basket beside it to create a more rustic look.

THE CIRCLE

AS THE WOMEN begin to arrive, greet and welcome them in whatever way feels natural to you.

Perhaps share some housekeeping notes with them, such as where the toilet is, where to put their bags, and of course a reminder to ensure their phones are off. I like to use this time to suggest that if they'd like to take pictures of the space they do so now, so that everyone can then fully disconnect from their phones.

You can then invite each Woman to find a cushion or space around the Circle to sit.

For some Circles, it may feel right to use this time to talk and catch up; for other Circles it may feel best to sit in silence as you wait for the Circle to open. A good way to gauge the best option is to pick up on the energy as everyone walks in, and to hold the space for whatever that energy is.

For example, if you notice people coming in a little frazzled, or stressed, or with heightened energy, you may encourage them to find a cushion to sit on, to close their eyes, and begin to tune in, in whatever way they need to. This may be a good time for them to let go of their day, and transition gently into the more grounded, nourishing energy of the Women's Circle.

Once everyone has gathered, it will be time to close the door and open the space.

So let's bring forward our Circle and dive deeper into all the aspects as we learn how to hold each part.

OPEN THE SPACE

Welcome

Once everyone has arrived and the Circle is whole, it is time to open the space. I do this by welcoming everyone into the Circle and sharing a brief introduction on what a Women's Circle is. I usually say something along the lines of:

'A Women's Circle is a safe and sacred space for Women to gather, a space of non-judgement, a space to come home to yourself and to see yourself in the reflection of each other.

This is a space to remember your power, and to support each other in remembering theirs.

The Circle is ancient, it is sacred, and by gathering with one another we reclaim this for ourselves and for all Women. Once a Circle opens it never closes, meaning we have all gathered here before, we have all sat in a Circle together once upon a lifetime ago.

So thank you for being here, thank you for hearing the call, thank you for stepping back into the Circle.'

You may want to elaborate on this, talking more deeply about the origins of the Women's Circle, or you may want to keep it brief. Trust where you are guided.

Once I have introduced the Women's Circle I then share the deeper intention as to why we are gathering. For example:

'We are gathering tonight to honour the new moon with the intention of setting some powerful intentions.'

SMUDGING

In order to activate the energy of the Circle, we must begin by cleansing the Women in the Circle, our altars, and the physical space.

Smudging is an ancient ritual that clears and cleanses the energy of the space and our own auric field before a ceremony begins. We smudge to lift off any stagnant or negative energy we may be carrying. This creates the perfect opportunity to arrive in the space cleansed and purified.

Light your cleansing tool of choice, let the smoke begin to rise, then begin walking around the Circle clockwise as you trace the smoke around the outline of each Woman's body. If you're using a smudge stick, ensure you have something like a shell to catch any embers that may fly off.

You can use a feather to spread the smoke further around the body, or just use your hands to waft the smoke and breathe.

Repeat this prayer:

'May that which no longer serves you, may that which is not yours, be gone, now.'

Once you have gone around each Woman in the space, come back to your seat and smudge yourself. You can then step towards the altar and take a moment to smudge the inner Circle. It is here that you can send your wish out for the Circle and ask to call in any angels, guides or beings of a high vibration to come and gather with you in the Circle too (only if that's your thing, of course).

Then, when you feel the smudging is complete, gently put out any residual embers in a fireproof bowl.

You will feel a shift of energy in the space already. The opening of the space sends the calling out to the universe that you've welcomed in the sacred, and each Woman will feel it.

ACTIVATE OWN ENERGY

Invite each Woman to activate their own energy into the space by going around the Circle sharing their name, their astrology sign (to get a sense of what vibrations are in the house) and something about how they're feeling or why they chose to gather in the Circle. You can choose what little question you invite them to share depending on what Circle you're holding. Once each Woman has spoken and shared their energy, the Circle has been cast.

Energy talk

Now it is time to tune into the energy we are creating in the space. Remember, you as the facilitator have spent a great deal of time and energy cultivating this space, so it's important that you share this with the other Women so they can feel it too. Depending on why you are gathering, you may want to share the reasons in more detail.

In the following chapters I have suggested a different energy talk for each Circle. You can use that as a guide, and then sprinkle anything else over it to fully and authentically portray the energy of the Circle you have created.

MEDITATION

Meditation creates the perfect opportunity to go inwards and connect within. The true medicine of the Circle will emerge when each Woman shows up as her true and authentic self, and allows the wisdom and magik within her to be witnessed and received in the space.

So often we spend our lives running from ourselves, never taking a moment to come back to stillness, to our breath, to the present. This perhaps is one of the deepest curses of our culture – the more we spend time outside of ourselves, the more we forget that all we are seeking lies within.

Leading a short meditation at the start of your Circle will support the Women in coming home to themselves.

Connecting to the breath is probably the most important aspect of the meditations. This will facilitate each Woman to come into the present moment, into the now, into all that is.

The meditations given throughout this book change slightly depending on the reason you are gathering. For most of the Circles, I have offered a short meditation with questions of contemplation weaved in to connect to the energy of the Circle. These range from basic meditations to deeper guided visualisations.

A guided visualisation is a meditation practice that invites you to go on a visual journey within yourself, inviting you to imagine a specific scene or setting. This prompts you to fall into your subconscious and access parts of yourself that you haven't been conscious of, or hidden messages and answers that you are seeking.

Use your most gentle, melodic voice to read the meditations out loud. One tip I learnt was to read very slowly; there is no rush. The more slowly you guide the Circle through the meditation, the deeper they will be able to go.

Of course, the meditations offered in the book are just guidelines. Once you feel confident, you will be able to create your own.

SHARING CIRCLE

Once you have led the Women inwards, it's now time to lead them outwards, for the magik of the Circle is found both within us and outside of us through the reflection of each other.

A sharing circle is a key part of the Women's Circle. It creates a safe container for all that is rising in each Woman to be shared and witnessed. It creates the space to be seen by one another; without judgement and without trying to fix or change what is occurring.

Throughout the book, I have offered prompts for each Circle that you can open the sharing circle with. You may want to leave a little bit of space between the prompts and the sharing for each Woman to sit with what's coming up for them, and perhaps to write down and explore inwardly the messages they are receiving.

The space to be gently seen and heard is so rare in our culture, for we have truly lost the art of listening.

To support the values of the sharing circle, you can begin by introducing the talking

stick. A talking stick is a tool used in Native American communities to determine who can speak during the Circle and when. Whoever is holding the talking stick is the only person with permission to speak – everyone else is there to hold the space. You can weave this practice into your Circle by decorating a wooden stick. Alternatively, I like to use a rose quartz crystal, and pass it around the Circle to each Woman as they share.

You can also introduce the practice of listening from the heart. Guide the Women to focus their attention and presence on each Woman as they speak, to truly witness them, hear them and observe their body language.

If you listen closely enough to your sisters, you may just find your own stories hidden in the layers of theirs.

Open the Circle by introducing the talking stick, and take this opportunity to invite anyone who feels called to share to begin. This can sometimes take a while, as it takes a brave one to begin the sharing.

As you wait, you can hold the space by creating a loving, accepting energy in the room. Of course, if you feel called, you can always begin by sharing something from your heart. This can be a beautiful way of softening the space, welcoming vulnerability and giving the other Women permission to share.

Not every Woman will feel the call to share, and that's totally okay. Honour each Woman's space as you begin to weave around. It's important to not put any pressure on anyone, but rather to continue creating a safe and sacred space for the Women who do want to share.

Once everyone who feels called to share has done so, you will again find the energy of the Circle has deepened. You have connected to a deeper layer of the Circle, and you will all be more connected than before.

PULLING CARDS

Using this deeper energy, we can now welcome in any further wisdom, or messages from the universe to support us with the intention for the Circle. We will do this by connecting to the universe through Oracle cards.

Oracle cards are a very direct way to communicate with the universe. Each card will hold a different frequency and energy, and can reveal deeper messages for us.

Before pulling the cards it's important to open everyone up to receiving them. To facilitate this, lead a short activating meditation, by inviting each Woman to close their eyes and rub their palms together until they feel a warmth, or tingling. As they feel the tingling, invite them to rub their hands a little harder, then harder again, until their arms feel like they're going to fall off. Then welcome them to begin separating their hands, and to take a moment to feel the energy they've created.

This is usually a really beautiful moment in the Circle, in which we remember the power we hold to create energy.

Once the Women feel their power, you can welcome the card question I have offered in each Circle, or you can use a generic one, such as:

'What message do I need to receive?'
'What do I need to be shown?'

Invite each Woman to hold that question in their heart.

Pass the deck around and ask each Woman to hold the deck in the palms of their hands, shuffling the deck as they repeat the question to themselves. When they feel called to, they can stop shuffling, pull the card they feel called to, and place that card face down. They can then pass the deck on to the Woman beside them.

Once everyone has pulled a card, you can invite the Women to turn the cards over, and guide them on how to read the cards for themselves.

READING CARDS

Each Oracle deck comes with a book explaining each card in deeper detail. However, I was always taught to let your intuition guide you first, for this is how we learn to trust our ability to commune with the universe, without relying on someone else to tell us what the cards are trying to say.

When reading cards, it's important to read from your heart rather than your head. In other words, stop trying to work out what the card means, and instead look at how it makes you feel. Take time to truly stare into the card, to become present to what's happening in the card, what colours, symbols, beings and words are there, and to tune into what you feel this card is revealing to you.

Once each Woman has sat with their card, you can go around the Circle, opening the space for each Woman to share her message and what she felt it was telling her. As you weave throughout the Circle, listen to all that each Woman shares, ensure you are still practicing listening from the heart. For you may just find that the Woman next to you has brought back a piece of wisdom for you too.

RITUAL

Now that you have received your messages from the Circle, it is time to seal these messages in through ritual. A ritual is the physical act of making something sacred. It is the perfect way to gather all the messages that have been created, shared or passed on in the Circle and to honour the intention that has unveiled itself to you.

Throughout this book I have given beautiful examples of all the rituals I've held for different Circles, with a full ingredients list and a basic how-to practice.

Please note: performing a ritual is a sacred act, and requires your presence and attention, both to yourself and to witness each other, as you physically embody the magik of the Circle. This is how you will call your dreams, visions and wishes for the Circle into being.

Once the Circle is ready to move into the ritual, I would typically perform the ritual first to show the other Women how to do it. This creates a nice flow and helps everyone to feel more comfortable in what they are about to embark on. I would then invite each Woman, one by one, to rise and go around the Circle clockwise performing theirs.

Giving each Woman the space to do her own ritual is really important because it means everyone isn't doing it at the same time. This creates an opportunity for the Women to witness each other.

Once you've finished your ritual, this will mark the journey of closing the Circle.

CLOSING THE CIRCLE

Before the Circle closes, I like to take a few moments to come back and ground into the Circle, to sit in and to feel the energy we've created in this space together.

The closing of the Circle creates a moment to acknowledge and honour all that has been, all that is and all that's to come.

I invite each Woman to return back to herself, by closing her eyes and giving thanks to herself for showing up, for stepping back into the Circle. I then invite her to give thanks to her sisters, who each gathered and witnessed her. Then, finally, to give thanks to the universe for all she revealed in the magik of the Circle.

I close some of my Circles by inviting each Woman to rise, gather their belongings and leave in sacred silence so that they can hold the energy created in the space for as long as possible.

However, if you plan to eat or be together, you can just gently welcome them back into the space and thank them all for gathering. And so it is.

POST-CIRCLE

Once everyone has left, it is important for you to nourish yourself. The energy will have been high, and you as facilitator have given much of yourself to this space, so ensuring you look after yourself is important.

Here are some tips on grounding your energy:

☾ Smudge yourself and the space once everyone leaves
☾ Soak in a ritual bath filled with salts and essential oils
☾ Take a walk barefoot in your garden (if you have one)
☾ Eat a nourishing meal
☾ Listen to some soothing music

All of the above will help your energy to settle, and will replenish you well after the Circle. I cannot stress enough the importance of taking care of yourself. You have facilitated the revival of the Circle, it is now time to honour yourself.

III

HOLDING YOUR CIRCLE

*   *   *

NATURE
NURTURE
RITES OF PASSAGE

NATURE

THE MOON • THE SUN • SEASONS

NOW THAT WE'VE gone through the basics of the Circle, we are going to be looking at how we can work with nature in order to support, guide and inspire our spaces. For the true magik of the Women's Circles lies in the deep knowing that we are co-creating the space alongside the universe. As such, getting to know nature and connecting to how it's communicating with you is the first step in welcoming its energy, its power and medicine into space.

I believe the sun, the moon, the stars and all the seasons are walking beside us, subtly guiding us throughout life. Every aspect of nature holds a unique energy that, once we are attuned to, we can consciously work with to support, inspire and draw the magik in our Circles.

THE MOON

FOR WHEN THE MOON STARTS CALLING YOU ...
THERE IS NOTHING TO DO BUT LISTEN.

The first type of Women's Circles I held were Moon Circles. Moon Circles are perhaps the most well-known type of gatherings. The memory of what the moon represents still ripples in all of us, and so the calling to gather during different phases of the moon feels so natural.

The beauty of the Moon Circle lies in the invitation to begin to connect and explore lunar energy in ways that most of us have never experienced before. Lunar energy is considered to be feminine, because its inner, mysterious and cyclical energy likens it to the Woman's path.

In ancient times, all calendars were lunar. We followed the moon as a way to gauge time – one moon cycle was equal to one moonth (or month, as we now know it). The moon was a powerful ally for small communities who had little or no way of connecting to the outside world. Studying the moon and its phases revealed when the waters were stirring, when the tides would rise, when the seasons would change. At a time where there were no street lights, the moon lit the way even in the darkest of nights. Basking in, honouring and dancing in the moonlight was seen as a sacred and necessary part of every cycle.

The farmers worked with the moon to know when to plant and harvest, and many farmers, even now, still plant seeds under a full moon, as this is known to be the most fertile time to plant.

The moon didn't just tell us what we needed to know about the outside world, it gave us the opportunity to tend to our inner world, too. Just as the moon controls the tides and the oceans outside of us, it also controls the waters within us – we are, after all, made up of almost 80 per cent water. So of course the moon stirs things up within us, boiling and bringing things to the surface. The moon talks to us, guiding us through its phases, revealing its energy as a way to help us reveal our own. The moon reminds us that we are nature.

We can understand this more deeply by studying the different phases the moon moves through. The more we work with the moon, the more it reveals to us. So let's go on a journey.

THE JOURNEY OF THE MOON

WE ONLY NEED TO STARE UP AT THE MOON
TO SEE HER PHASES REFLECTED IN US.
AS JUST AS SHE WAXES AND WANES,
WE SOON REALISE SO DO WE.

Tip Buy or create a moon calendar.
This can be a beautiful way to connect to the moon and her cycles.
Each month, note down what dates the new, full and dark moon fall upon,
as you start to connect to how her phases affect your own.

The new moon is the phase that marks the beginning of the lunar cycle. This is an opportunity to start again, to be reborn. A new moon represents the welcoming of fresh energy, the seeds of potential, the hope of what lies ahead. As we welcome the new moon, we begin a journey of twenty-nine days, watching as she waxes, growing day by day, until she reaches her fullness.

The full moon marks the moment when we are met with the brightest light of the month. The moon is at her fullest, and she shines her light down onto us amid the darkness of the night sky. The moon is in full bloom, abundant, reflective and in her glory.

Once she meets her fullness, she then gracefully begins to let go and follows the journey back to the dark; waning, releasing her light day after day, gently letting go.

The dark moon marks the moment where her light disappears into the dark of the night sky. It is here that she has to let go in order to be reborn again.

As you step back and listen to the ancient cycles of the moon, I wonder, do you hear the cycles within you start to stir?

For the journey the moon takes each month is the very same journey that we take. If we look at our inner cyclical rhythms, we will see them mirrored back to us through the moon's gaze.

There is a new wave of Women who are spreading this work far and wide. They are referring to their menstruation as their 'moon time', as a way to acknowledge and honour the cycles and phases, and the deep connection we have to the moon.

In ancient times, Women lived in small, intimate communities. Not only would all the Women's cycles align, they typically aligned with the phases of the moon too. So it was easy to see the parallels, and easier to understand how intertwined we were to nature, to what we were being asked to honour both within and outside of us, and just how magikal we as Women are!

This is why Women would gather on a new moon, a full moon, or a dark moon, harnessing the energy of each phase. Women knew they could commune with the moon to support both their inner and outer worlds.

When we begin to collect and gather around the moon cycles, we begin to realise how deeply we are connected to her, and how much magik she has to give to us. Once we remember the moon, she begins to work with us in the most wonderful of ways.

So this is a calling, to connect back to the moon, to work with her magik, to understand the opportunities she gives us each month to begin again, to reflect and to release. Remember, in honouring her phases, you begin to honour your own.

MOON CIRCLES

Moon Circles are sacred spaces created around the phases of the moon. During the month, you can gather at each phase of the moon, or just pick one phase to hold your Circle in.

You will be amazed how by working with the moon, you begin to co-create a space with her. She will provide you with all the energy you need to create the most powerful space.

DID YOU KNOW
THE FULL MOON TALKS TO YOU
WHISPERING WORDS
THROUGHOUT THE DAY,

DID YOU KNOW
THAT IF YOU LISTEN CLOSE ENOUGH,
YOU MIGHT JUST HEAR
WHAT SHE HAS TO SAY.

STARING UP AT HER,
AS YOU SEE HER FULLNESS,
HER LIGHT IS WHAT WILL GUIDE THE WAY.

GENTLY, SISTER, AS YOU GO,
THIS IS WHAT SHE BEGINS TO SAY.

ALL THAT'S NEEDED IS TO TAKE ONE STEP,
AND TO KNOW THAT
EVERYTHING IS GOING TO BE OKAY.

FOR YOU WON'T REACH
THE TOP OF THE MOUNTAIN BY
TRYING TO GET THERE,
BUT RATHER BY TAKING IN
WHAT YOU SEE ALONG YOUR WAY.

IT'S TIME TO COME HOME TO YOURSELF,
TO STEP BACK TO ALL YOU'VE
KNOWN SINCE THAT FIRST DAY.
THAT YOU ARE HELD, YOU ARE GUIDED,
YOU ARE LOVED IN EVERY WAY.

SURRENDER, SWEET GIRL,
THERE IS NOTHING TO RUSH.
FOR YOU, MY DARLING,
ARE ON YOUR WAY,

THE LIGHT IN ME IS THE LIGHT IN YOU.
THIS IS WHAT SHE HAD TO SAY.

THE NEW MOON CIRCLE

Setting new intentions

On the new moon, or up to three days after it

WHO

Gather three or more Women who are hearing the calling to gather on the new moon

GATHER

+ ritual basket
+ 1 × bunch of seasonal flowers (one stem for every Woman)
+ 3 × clear quartz crystals
+ 1 × craft tag per Woman
+ a pinch of anything else you feel called to bring in

ALTAR

Lay down your ritual cloth and begin to create your flower circle, taking the stems from your seasonal bunch to form the mandala. (Keep the flower heads on for this flower circle, as you will be gifting each Woman a flower stem in the ritual.)

Place tea lights in between the spaces created. Intentionally place your clear quartz crystals in the Circle too. Keep your ritual basket close to you, as you will need to draw on it during the gathering.

OPEN THE SPACE

Introduce yourself, the practice of the Women's Circle and the intention behind why you are gathering. Smudge the Women clockwise, then yourself, and then finally the altar space. Invite each Woman to introduce themselves, to share why they were drawn to gather and how they are feeling in this moment.

ENERGY TALK

This is the perfect time to gather, to set new intentions for the month ahead. The moon is empty and receptive at this moment and is open to your dreams, wishes and visions if you should give her time to connect.

This is a super potent moment to tell the moon your dreams and watch as, just like the moon, they grow into fullness.

MEDITATION

Invite the Circle to close their eyes, taking three deep inhalations, in through the nose and out through the mouth. Invite them to ground into the earth beneath them as they settle into this sacred space.

Ask that they begin to visualise a bright white light in their mind's eyes, and welcome them to feel this bright white light as it begins to flood their inner being. Starting from the crown of their head, down the eyes, nose, mouth, chin. Feeling it fall down their throat, shoulders, arms, hands. Into their chest, solar plexus, stomach and womb. Welcome this bright white light into their thighs, legs, ankles, all the way down to the soles of their feet.

Welcome the light of the new moon into your being, asking that it brings forward that we are ready to welcome into our own lives and trusting that it will be so.

Very gently, bring the Circle back into the room, infused with new moon energy that will guide you through the rest of the Circle.

SHARING PROMPTS

As the new moon rises, we prepare to go on a new journey, a new walk around the moon cycle. Begin to lead the sharing circle by asking a few questions and creating space for each Woman to write down what comes to her: What is it you dream of for this new month ahead?

+ What are you ready to call into your life? This can be something physical, mental, emotional or spiritual.
+ What do you vision for yourself?
+ Once you feel everyone is ready, open the space up for sharing.

ORACLE CARDS

Pull some cards to connect to the energy of Mama Moon, asking for guidance on what energy or piece of wisdom you may need to bring forth this new wish. Depending on what you have already received, you can ask any of these questions to gain a deeper clarity:

+ What may I need to know in order to bring forward my new moon intention?
+ What might I need to let go of in order to call in my new moon intention?
+ What might I need to believe in order to attract this new moon wish?

RITUAL

Hand out the craft tags, and one by one write your new moon intentions onto them. This can be your new moon wish, anything you need to let go of and anything you need to call in. Write these down with intention, and when you're ready, place the cards on the ritual cloth.

Then, one by one, guide each Woman to step into the Circle, pick up their intention card and a flower they feel drawn to, then walk around the Circle three times before returning to their seat.

Each Woman should then place the stem and the card together in their palms in prayer and raise them up to the new moon, ready to be received, answered and held by the spirit.

They can then gently bring their palms back to their chest, open their eyes, and sit back down in the Circle.

Wait until each Woman has risen and set their intentions to the new moon.

CLOSE THE CIRCLE

You will then close the space, perhaps by inviting everyone to close their eyes as they send gratitude to themselves, the Women around them and the new moon.

POST-CIRCLE

A nice action to take is to encourage the Women to sleep beside their flowers and intention cards. They could even place the cards under their pillows until the full moon as a reminder of all that they have wished upon this month.

THE FULL MOON CIRCLE

A time to give gratitude and manifest

On the full moon, or up to three days before or after it

WHO

Three or more Women who feel called to gather on the full moon

GATHER

- ✦ ritual basket
- ✦ a full moon offering (seasonal flowers, herbs or food), making sure there is enough for each Woman to have one of her own
- ✦ 1 × crystal you feel drawn to

Invite each Woman to bring one crystal that she feels drawn to.

ALTAR

Lay down the ritual cloth, creating a full moon offering spread with the herbs, flowers or food you gathered. Place your crystal within the circle and dot tea lights throughout.

OPEN THE SPACE

Introduce yourself, the practice of the Women's Circle and the intention behind why you are gathering. Smudge the Women clockwise, then yourself, and then finally the altar space. Invite each Woman to introduce themselves, to share why they were drawn to gather and how they are feeling in this moment. You can then welcome them to place their crystal on the altar space.

ENERGY TALK

The full moon is a time to pause. Midway through the month, we are guided by the light of the moon to stare up into the night sky and to connect to what she is shining back to you.

What is she asking you to see? This is such a potent time to gather, to really allow yourself to tune into the messages she is sending you. The moon is full, and is longing to communicate with you.

MEDITATION

Invite the Circle to close their eyes, taking three deep inhalations, in through the nose and out through the mouth. Invite them to ground into the earth beneath them as they settle into this sacred space.

Welcome in the energy of the full moon by inviting the Circle to pause, to step away from their thoughts, to-do lists and busyness, and to come back to the stillness of this very moment.

Can you bring forward one thing you are truly grateful for in this moment, and just take a few moments to feel your gratitude as it pulses through your entire being?

Visualise the thing you are most grateful for. Breathe into it, send love to all that it is giving you, to all that it has given you and to all that you believe it will give you.

It is with this energy of gratitude that we can manifest all that we are calling into our lives. For gratitude is the key to opening the doors of our dreams.

Gently guide the Women back to their bodies, reset with the energy of gratitude as you arrive back in the Circle.

SHARING PROMPTS

Begin to lead the sharing circle by asking a few questions and creating space for each Woman to write down what comes to her:

+ How are you feeling at this moment?
+ What has been triggering you the past few days?
+ What is coming up to the surface?
+ What did you feel most grateful for in the meditation?
+ What do you feel the full moon is asking you to see?

Remember: listen to your sisters' words, for they will be mirroring back all you need to hear, and their words may just hold your message from the moon too.

ORACLE CARDS

Pull some cards to connect to the energy of the Mama Moon. Ask for guidance on what energy or piece of wisdom you may need in order to manifest and to feel a deeper sense of gratitude for what is.

Depending on what you have already received, you can ask any of these questions to gain a deeper clarity:

✦ What is the best use of my energy on this full moon?
✦ What might I need to let go of in order to manifest all that I'm seeking?
✦ Where might I need to bring a deeper sense of gratitude into my life?

Encourage each Woman to connect to all the messages they've been sent from the moon – what has the moon revealed to them tonight? What does it want them to see reflected through its gaze? Each Woman should write down anything that has come up.

They can then gather the crystal they brought from the altar space. If you're inside, step outside with all your sisters. Whether you're in a garden, a street, a balcony or a beach; whether the moonlight is visible or masked by clouds, it doesn't matter. The moon is always there, even when it seems to be hiding.

Standing under the dark night sky in a circle, holding hands with the Women beside you under the light of the full moon, close your eyes and feel its energy. Bathe in its light.

Send gratitude for all it has revealed to you tonight, for all the messages it has sent you.

Have each Woman place their crystal in their palm and raise their hands up to the dark night sky as they seal Mama Moon's messages into the crystal.

CLOSE THE CIRCLE

Come back to the Circle, grounding back into the sacredness of the space you've created. Close your eyes as you take a moment to send gratitude to yourself, to the Women who gathered beside you and to Mama Moon.

POST-CIRCLE

When they get home, each Woman can place her crystal outside all night to further charge it under the moon. In the morning, she can collect her charged crystal, which will now be infused with the energy, wisdom and messages she received from the Women's Circle.

THE DARK MOON CIRCLE

Release and let go of negative energy

On the dark moon, or up to three days before it

WHO

Three or more sisters who are hearing the calling to gather on the dark moon

GATHER

- ✦ ritual basket
- ✦ 1 × tea light per Woman gathering
- ✦ 1 × fireproof pot

ALTAR

Lay down your ritual cloth and create a circle from the tea lights –
don't light them, as they will be a part of the ritual. Place the pillar candle
in the centre of the circle, which you can light.

OPEN THE SPACE

Introduce yourself, the practice of the Women's Circle and the intention
behind why you are gathering. Smudge the Women clockwise, then yourself,
and then finally the altar space. Invite each Woman to light a tea light in the
circle and to introduce themselves, to share why they were drawn to gather
and how they are feeling in this moment.

ENERGY TALK

The energy at this time is calling us to be still, to feel, to cleanse, to purify, to release. It's a time to gather, to shift energy, and release what no longer serves us.

As we gather here to invoke the energy of the dark moon, allowing and welcoming her darkness to envelop us, we go on a journey to uncover what she is asking us to see. Remembering that it is only in stepping towards the dark that we find its wisdom.

MEDITATION

The dark moon is an opportune time to sit with all that is, so once you've shared, perhaps this is a moment to welcome in the silence.

To sit with what it is, sit in silence, welcoming in the darkness, welcoming in the space to be with it, knowing that within the dark moon holds the energy to welcome the dark and alchemise it. Invite each Woman to close their eyes, consciously welcoming them on a journey into darkness. Guide them to focus on their breath as they become more deeply aware of the darkness within.

Invite them to welcome anything that's been challenging them, to rise up to the surface to be seen. When they return from the meditation, invite them to bring forth their tea light from the altar space and place it beside them as a way to remind themselves that they hold the power to alchemise and transform their darkness into light.

SHARING PROMPTS

Begin to lead the sharing circle by asking a few of the questions below and creating space for each Woman to write down what comes to her:

+ What came through in the meditation?
+ Was it uncomfortable to sit in the dark?
+ Could you feel into any shadows that have been lurking?
+ What's been triggering you this month?
+ What fears or negative chatter have emerged?
+ What have you been distracting yourself from?
+ What are you being called to let go of?

Give each Woman the space to be with what is, and when you feel ready, open up the space for sharing.

77

ORACLE CARDS

Pull some cards to connect to the energy of the dark moon, asking for guidance from the moon on anything you are being called to release or let go of.

+ What am I being called to let go of this dark moon?
+ What else do I need to know?

RITUAL

Guide each Woman to write down what they are ready to release on a piece of paper; tuning into all that the Circle has revealed to them about what they need to let go of.

One by one, each Woman can read all that they're ready to let go of out loud, then release the paper into their tea light. As they do, encourage them to watch how the light they spark will alchemise the darkness.

Witness each Woman as they take turns to release what's no longer serving them, for witnessing each other is such a gift. Remembering that when one Woman heals, she also heals the Women before her and after her.

What a privilege to watch a Woman finding their way, amid the darkness of the dark moon.

CLOSE THE CIRCLE

Gently invite each Woman to close her eyes, returning back to the darkness within, bringing a sense of gratitude for what the darkness revealed, and knowing that you hold the torch to journey through the dark. Send gratitude to yourself for embarking on the quest, to your sisters for holding the space and to the dark moon for creating the gateway.

The dark moon is here calling us gently into the darkness,
beckoning us forward, asking us to stay a while.

We've been conditioned to be so afraid of the dark,
so when we are pulled in, which inevitably we all are at some point,
we spend our time and energy seeking the exit route
rather than falling into the process.

We find anything in our power to take us out of the present moment,
to numb the dark, or bring a false light
to it in the hope that all will fade away.

But what if you are exactly where you're meant to be?
A wise Woman once told me in a time of struggle
that the only way is through.

So what if we could all reframe the darkness,
what if it wasn't so scary to sit with all the discomfort,
what if that was in fact the very way out?

As the darkness comes forward,
this creates the perfect opportunity to sit in a circle,
and allow for all that is waiting to transform
to be done with reverence, stillness and grace.

For if we are the only way out of the darkness,
can we sit in the process,
supporting each other as we allow
the deep transformation we are being called to, to unfold?

THE SUN

IF THE MOON IS FEMININE,
THEN THE SUN, ITS OPPOSITE, IS MASCULINE.

Linear instead of cyclical, focused and directional rather than fluid and receptive, the sun illuminates what you can already see. It brings forth the energy to move towards all that is waiting for you.

The solar cycle is 365 days and moves into a different astrological sign every thirty days. Each sign holds its own unique energy and vibration. The sun and the stars have so much to tell us, so much to reveal to us. Like the moon – we need to pay attention.

In ancient times we looked to the cosmos for guidance. The positioning of certain planets, the studies of stars, the configuration of constellations, would all reveal and inform us on things in our lives; they called this astrology.

Nowadays, we've lost touch with this divine communication. Here, we will explore how we can weave each sign into our lives and into our Circles.

Astrology is a language that allows the sky to speak to you; there is nothing more magical than that.

I learnt about the sun and its energy by walking consciously through the year. I was guided by a witch I met on my travels. She took me under her wing and taught me about the stars and the planets, the signs and the placements, not through any textbooks or teachings, but simply by getting out in nature and walking. Each time the sun entered a new sign, we would go out into the woods and notice the frequency and energy of this shift.

What did nature look like at this time? What were the animals doing? What colours were all around us? How did it feel in our bodies to be in this new sign?

I realised you could learn so much not by studying what it all meant, but just purely by living it. It reminded me that all of nature's teachings are right here in front of us. For the sun reveals life to us, it lights up both the good and bad, the light and the shadows. When you consciously learn to connect to the sun and all the gifts it gives us throughout the year, you live in harmony with the life force of energy, both within and outside of you. Every month as we move into a new sign, we can work with that sign's unique energy to weave its wisdom, teachings and magik into our Circles.

ARIES CIRCLE

Connect to your inner child

21 March – 20 April

WHO

Three or more Women

GATHER

- ✦ ritual basket
- ✦ 1 × large bunch of seasonal flowers (daffodils, yellow flowers or any seasonal offering you forage from nature)

ALTAR

Lay down your ritual cloth. Create a small circle of tea lights in the centre, then create a larger flower circle by placing your seasonal flowers in a circle around the tea lights.

OPEN THE SPACE

Introduce yourself, the practice of the Women's Circle and the intention behind why you are gathering. Smudge the Women clockwise, then yourself, and then finally the altar space. Invite each Woman to introduce themselves and their astrology sign, and to share why they were drawn to gather and how they are feeling at this moment.

ENERGY TALK

Aries is the spark that lives within, the spark you were born with, your innate essence. During the sign of Aries we are given the perfect opportunity to create a sacred space that will aid in welcoming us back to this energy. As we sit in this circle of flickering lights, we remember the spark within. As we sit bathing in this youthful, childlike energy, we invoke our inner child to come forth. Let us allow Aries to journey us back to who we truly are ... while giving us the fire and spirit to step towards it.

MEDITATION

Invite the Circle to close their eyes and take three deep inhalations, in through the nose and out through the mouth.

Visualise yourself journeying into a beautiful meadow. The air is crisp, the sun is just starting to rise, and you begin to awaken and step out into a quiet and serene wild meadow.

Everything is beginning to wake up. The grass is green, the daffodils are trumpeting and the baby lambs are playing in the distance. The grass is dewy and as the sun rises it graces your face and leaves a subtle tingling on your skin.

You begin to explore this beautiful landscape that you're in, noticing the colours you see, the smells you smell and any more animals that may appear.

As the sun rises, you stare into it, taking it all in. As the sun gets brighter and brighter you stare deeper and deeper into its light ... and notice, within the bright sunlight, the outline of a small girl.

She is surrounded by the light of the sun, a golden light ... she is your inner child. Take her in; she joyfully begins to step out of the sunlight and approaches you.

She is here to remind you of your true essence, of your inner joy. She begins to call to you to show you what she loves to do. She takes you by the hand and begins to play. What does she want to play with you? What is it that she loves to do? How does it feel being around her? What energy does she hold?

Take her in, listen to what she has to say, watch what she loves to do. Allow yourself to play with her as you spend time just being, just connecting, just remembering this beautiful, playful, innocent part of you; the spark within.

You ask her what you need to know in order to awaken this spark within you in your everyday life. Listen to what she has to say. She may do something, say something, or show you something ... let her guide you.

Before you leave her, she flicks you a spark of the sunlight, placing it in your hands. You take this time to thank her for helping you remember, then you watch as slowly she returns. And with that, you feel the spark within you, as you begin to gently feel yourself returning back to your physical body, to the Circle as you open your eyes filled with the light of her.

SHARING PROMPTS

Begin to lead the sharing circle by asking a few questions and creating space for each Woman to write down what comes to her:

+ What did you love to do as a child?
+ When and why did you stop doing it?
+ What are you being called to reawaken in your life?
+ What brave step can you take in your own life to move towards your true passions?

Open up the sharing circle by inviting each Woman to share what came through.

ORACLE CARDS

Shuffle the deck then pass the cards around, inviting each Woman to connect to the spirit of the sun in Aries. Each Woman should set the intention to receive some deeper guidance and wisdom as they connect to its energy.

+ Is there any other message your inner child has for you?
+ Is there anything she'd like you to know or remember?

Guide the Women to share the cards they received and the message they felt their card gave them.

RITUAL

Invite each Woman to stare into the fire circle in the middle of the altar space, reminding them of that inner spark within.

Guide them to write down on a piece of paper what part of their inner child is ready to come through and shine.

One by one, the Women can collect a flower of their choice and, holding this flower in their palms, step over the fire circle and whisper their wish into the flames, sealing the spark into the flower.

As each Woman returns back to their seat, they invite the next Woman to rise.

CLOSE THE CIRCLE

Once everyone has returned back to the Circle, invite each Woman to close their eyes, holding their flower, as they take a moment to honour their inner child for guiding them on this journey, sending gratitude to all the sisters who gathered and to the energy of Aries for lighting the way.

POST-CIRCLE

Invite each Woman to keep the flower close by for the whole month of Aries. Let it be a reminder of the spark within them, the spark that is ready to be seen.

TAURUS CIRCLE

Tend to all that needs nourishing within

22 April – 21 May

WHO

Three or more Women

GATHER

- ✦ ritual basket
- ✦ 1 × bucket of soil (enough for each Woman to fill a small plant pot)
- ✦ 1 × bunch of roses
- ✦ 1 × rose essential oil or incense stick

Invite each Woman to bring a small plant pot and some seeds of their choice (my tip would be something that's easy to grow inside, such as tomato or a herb).

ALTAR

Lay down your ritual cloth and centre the bucket of soil in the middle. Create a flower circle around the bucket using your roses; you may feel called to just use her petals. Dot the candles around the circle, and place your ritual basket beside it. You can burn your rose essential oil or incense stick on the altar space too.

OPEN THE SPACE

Introduce yourself, the practice of the Women's Circle and the intention behind why you are gathering. Smudge the Women clockwise, then yourself, and then finally the altar space. Invite each Woman to introduce themselves, their astrology sign, why they felt the calling to gather, and the seed they brought with them. Invite them to place their pots and seeds onto the altar space once they've introduced themselves.

ENERGY TALK

Taurus is Mother Earth itself. During the Circle in the sign of Taurus, we are given an opportunity to connect to this grounding energy. As we create a sensual space, weaving in blossoming smells and seasonal flowers, we allow ourselves to fall back into the arms of Taurus. We use this Circle as a way to activate the parts of us that need tending, the parts of us that need to remember how to hold ourselves, in a gentle, loving and nourishing way.

MEDITATION

This meditation is a beautiful opportunity to connect back to where, within you, you need nourishment and tending. Use the breath to go on a journey within, as you connect to the parts of you that are in need of Taurean nourishment.

Guide the Circle to close their eyes and take three deep inhalations, in through the nose and out through the mouth. Then invite them to visualise themselves stepping into an enchanted woodland.

It's morning time, the rabbits are out, and the birds are tweeting. Bluebells cover the land.

You see an old wooden gate and push it open, entering a secret garden. There is a place to leave your shoes so you can walk barefoot on the grass. Notice how it feels to have your feet on the earth, and to feel safe, supported and held by the ground beneath you.

You begin to explore the landscape, noticing what flowers surround you. What smells do you smell? What do you see? Allow yourself to explore this secret enchanted garden.

In the distance you notice a friendly woodland animal beginning to approach you ... what animal has journeyed to you?

The animal tells you it's here to support you, and asks you what you need in this moment to feel grounded. What do you need to receive in order to feel nourished? What do you need to nurture yourself right now? Allow a message to rise from within you.

The animal knows that you must feel nourished in order to grow; you must feel safe in order to receive. You are given some seeds to plant. With your bare hands you take these seeds and begin to plant your intention into the earth of the secret garden, sowing any wishes you have, any dreams you long for into Mother Earth.

When you are ready, thank the animal for its love and guidance, as you journey back into the woodland, and prepare to journey back to your physical body.

SHARING PROMPTS

Begin to lead the sharing circle by asking a few questions and creating space for each Woman to write down what comes to her:

+ What is longing to be tended to within?
+ Where do you need to nurture and nourish yourself more?
+ Where have you been neglecting yourself?

Once you feel called to, open the sharing circle, inviting each Woman to share something that came through in her journey and her responses to the sharing prompts.

ORACLE CARDS

Shuffle the deck then pass the cards around, inviting each Woman to connect to the spirit of the sun in Taurus. Each Woman should set the intention to receive some deeper guidance and wisdom as they connect to its energy.

+ What needs tending within?
+ What do I need in order to feel nourished?
+ What dreams are ready to be sown?

Guide the Women to share the cards they received and the message they felt their card gave them.

RITUAL

To connect to all the messages received in the Circle, invite each Woman to gather their seeds in the palms of their hands. One by one, stepping over to the altar space with her plant pot, each Woman takes a handful of soil in her bare hands and begins to plant her seeds.

With every action she takes, she is sealing her intention deeper into it, sowing her messages into the plant before returning back to her seat.

CLOSE THE CIRCLE

Once each Woman has planted her seeds, welcome the Women back to the Circle. Guide them to close their eyes as they take a moment to themselves, to reconnect back to all that they need, to the Women gathered beside them and to the energy of Taurus.

POST-CIRCLE

Invite the Women to take their plant pot home, water it, nurture it, sing to it. Let it be a loving reminder of all that you need to bring to yourself.

GEMINI CIRCLE

Remember your authentic voice

22 May – 21 June

WHO

Three or more Women

GATHER

- ✦ ritual basket
- ✦ 1 × incense stick (scent of your choice)
- ✦ 1 × bunch of seasonal flowers
- ✦ a handful of crystals you feel drawn to

ALTAR

Lay down your ritual cloth and begin to create your flower circle using the seasonal flowers. Drop your crystals within the spaces. Place a piece of paper and pen at each place within the circle. Keep the ritual basket beside the altar and light some beautiful incense.

OPEN THE SPACE

Introduce yourself, the practice of the Women's Circle and the intention behind why you are gathering. Smudge the Women clockwise, then yourself, and then finally the altar space. Invite each Woman to introduce themselves and their astrology sign, and to share why they felt the calling to gather and how they have been feeling.

ENERGY TALK

Gemini is a free spirit, flying through the sky, unpinned. It seeks to learn, to remember, to seek out new experiences. Working with this versatile energy, we are welcomed into an energetically fresh space that helps our minds to be free. This space is about reconnecting to our truth in order to remember what we really want and how to manifest it.

MEDITATION

Invite the Circle to close their eyes and take three deep inhalations, in through the nose and out through the mouth. Then invite them to visualise themselves in a room in a house.

A beautiful carpet sits on the floor; a magic carpet. Sitting on the carpet, you prepare to take flight, leaving the room you're in as you begin to visualise yourself flying through the sky.

Looking down from above, you see the place where you are, the town, the city, the country. As you fly deeper and deeper into the sky, everything gets smaller and smaller.

You realise that you in fact have wings, and when it feels safe to do so, you take a deep breath, looking at your wings and trusting ... as you begin to fly.

Feeling the cold air on your face, the freshness all around you, breathe it all in. How does it feel to fly? To see things from another perspective? Perhaps you see some friendly birds. What do they look like?

As you spend this time flying through the sky, I invite you to begin to bring into your mind's eye all you have been spending your time thinking about. For thoughts become actions, and actions become our reality.

What are you manifesting in your life simply by thinking about it all the time?

Can you see it playing out before your eyes? Do you really want that?

Do your heart and your higher self want that? Is it in alignment with who you are? Is it what you really want?

Allow yourself to see all that you have been manifesting in your life, and ask for some inspiration on how you could manifest this in a more aligned way. What might you need to do?

Listen, feel, experience ... Once you feel you've received all you've needed to, you can thank the sky and the birds for giving you this newfound perspective, then fly back through the window, into the room that you gathered in. Feel yourself gently returning back to your physical body, and back into this sacred space.

SHARING PROMPTS

Begin to lead the sharing circle by asking a few questions and creating space for each Woman to write down what comes to her:

✦ What is it that you truly want to manifest?
✦ What fears, beliefs or blocks are getting in the way of this manifestation coming through?
✦ What actionable step can you take towards your dream?

Once you feel called to, open the sharing circle, inviting each Woman to share something that came through in her journey and her responses to the sharing prompts.

ORACLE CARDS

Shuffle the deck then pass the cards around, inviting each Woman to connect to the spirit of the sun in Gemini. Each Woman should set the intention to receive some deeper guidance and wisdom as they connect to its energy.

✦ What am I being called to manifest?
✦ What may I need to stop believing in order to step towards it?

Guide the Women to share the cards they received and the message they felt their card gave them.

RITUAL

Invite the Women to gather a piece of paper and a pen from the altar space.

Tuning into all the messages you received, write down what you are being called to manifest.

Using the energy of Gemini, we will use our voices and our words to call this in.

For words are like spells, and within a sacred circle they hold so much power.

Once you have written down your manifestations, each Woman will rise one by one and speak or sing their wish out into the ether. Let it be held by spirit.

CLOSE THE CIRCLE

Once each Woman has spoken their manifestation, invite them to close their eyes as they take a moment to thank themselves for tuning into their power, to honour the Women who gathered beside them and to send gratitude to the energy of Gemini. And so it is.

POST-CIRCLE

Invite each Woman, every morning, to speak or sing their wish into reality, believing it is already so.

CANCER CIRCLE

Uncover your inner mother

21 June – 22 July

WHO

Three or more Women

GATHER

- ✦ ritual basket
- ✦ 1 × jug of filtered/sacred water collected from a holy spring
- ✦ a selection of moonstones, shells and white flowers to create a beautiful mandala
- ✦ 1 × mason jar for yourself
- ✦ jasmine essential oil

Invite each Woman to bring one small mason jar with them.

ALTAR

Lay down your ritual cloth and place the jug of water in the centre, then create your mandala of moonstones, shells and white flowers around it. Place your ritual basket close by.

OPEN THE SPACE

Introduce yourself, the practice of the Women's Circle and the intention behind why you are gathering. Smudge the Women clockwise, then yourself, and then finally the altar space. Invite each Woman to introduce themselves and their astrology sign, and to share why they felt the calling and how they are feeling.

ENERGY TALK

When working with the energy of Cancer, we are asked to call in the inner mother. This is a time to dive deep into the emotional cells of our being, to cleanse, to wash and to rinse off any emotional residue we may be carrying ... and to remember that deep within our own waters lies the eternal mother who is always holding, carrying and caring for us. Use this time to connect to her, and all that she is trying to show you.

MEDITATION

Invite the Circle to close their eyes and take three deep inhalations, in through the nose and out through the mouth. Gently welcome them to visualise themselves on a beautiful beach.

The sun is shining, casting a beautiful glittery path through the waves. You begin to follow the path. You step into the ocean, feeling the water as it washes over your body, until you are entirely submerged. You begin to float on the surface of the ocean, feeling the water support you. Knowing you are held, you are safe, can you surrender a little bit more into the arms of the ocean? Can you breathe a little deeper? Can you let go just an inch more? In this moment, just check in with how you feel. Can you fully allow yourself to be held? Perhaps this is the first time in a long time that you've just let go.

Notice any emotions that begin to rise up, allowing them to come to the surface. Any emotions, thoughts or feelings you've been holding onto, allow them to rise, knowing you are safe in these healing waters.

As they rise, simply allow them to be there as you feel a maternal presence holding them. You begin to feel not just the water supporting you, but loving arms wrapping around you. The arms of the divine mother. She is here to hold you; not to fix you. To welcome any feelings or emotions that are present.

For the mother reminds us that all she has to do is simply be there, to witness, to hold space, to welcome you back into her arms. Allow yourself this gift, as you gently feel rocked by the ocean.

Before you re-emerge out of this healing space, allow a message from the divine mother to rise up. What do you need to do in order to feel mothered? Wait until you receive a feeling, a word, a visual, a message from within. Once you receive this you can begin to thank the oceans and the divine mother for holding you.

Gently, you begin to emerge through the waters; feel yourself stepping back onto that beach, as you slowly begin to journey back into your physical body, arriving back in the sacred circle.

SHARING PROMPTS

Begin to lead the sharing circle by asking a few questions and creating space for each Woman to write down what comes to her:

- What emotions rose up for you?
- What is in need of holding?
- What message, if any, did you receive from your inner mother?
- How are you being asked to hold this for yourself?

Once you feel called to, open the sharing circle, inviting each Woman to share something that came through in her journey and her responses to the sharing prompts.

ORACLE CARDS

Shuffle the deck then pass the cards around, inviting each Woman to connect to the spirit of the sun in Cancer. Each Woman should set the intention to receive some deeper guidance and wisdom as they connect to its energy.

- What does the divine mother want you to know?
- How are you being called to mother yourself?

Guide the Women to share the cards they received and the message they felt their card gave them.

RITUAL

Connect to the messages you received, and guide each Woman to set an intention on how she is going to mother herself this month.

One by one, each Woman can step over to the altar space with their mason jar, pour some water from the jug into their jar, and whisper the ways she is ready to mother herself into the water.

They then place three drops of the jasmine essential oil into the jar as they seal their wishes into it.

Stepping back to their seat, each Woman holds their jar as they infuse their wishes into the Mama water. Once every Woman has created their Mama water, anoint yourselves in the space between your eyebrows with your water, as together you invoke the Mama within to rise.

CLOSE THE CIRCLE

Once you have all anointed yourselves, close your eyes, taking a moment to send gratitude to yourselves for the willingness to connect to the mother within you. Send gratitude to all the Women who gathered beside you, and finally to the energy of Cancer for guiding the way. And so it is.

POST-CIRCLE

Invite the Women to take their Mama water home with them and anoint, bathe or shower with a bit of the water every day, to remind them of what they need in order to feel held.

LEO CIRCLE

Discover your light and bask in it

23 July – 22 August

WHO

Three or more Women

GATHER

+ ritual basket
+ 1 × sunflower per Woman gathering
+ any other crystals or seasonal offerings you feel called to
+ 1 × craft tag per Woman

ALTAR

Lay down your ritual cloth and place your pillar candle in the centre.
Then create a flower circle using the sunflowers (don't take the heads
off as you will be offering the sunflower to each Woman as a gift).
Dot any crystals or seasonal offerings you feel called to into the altar.
Keep your ritual basket close by.

OPEN THE SPACE

Introduce yourself, the practice of the Women's Circle and the intention
behind why you are gathering. Smudge the Women clockwise, then yourself,
and then finally the altar space. Invite each Woman to introduce themselves
and their astrology sign, and to share why they felt the calling to gather and
one thing they like about themselves.

ENERGY TALK

To bask in the light of you who you are is the energy that Leo calls us towards. What a glorious time to gather, to reconnect back to our own glory and to reveal it to others in a safe and sacred space. For this is our time to remember our light and to shine it outwards. This is our time to sit in a golden space, filled with joy and light ... Let us go on a journey of remembering.

MEDITATION

Invite the Circle to close their eyes and take three deep inhalations, in through the nose and out through the mouth.

It's time to go on a journey. Guide the Women to begin by visualising themselves on a hot summer's day, stepping out into a glorious field of sunflowers.

Watch as the sunflowers stand tall, shining their heads towards you as they welcome you to bask in their glorious field. You begin to walk through and with each step you take, you feel yourself rising higher and higher. Your back straightens, your head sits high, and you begin to allow any insecurities you've been harbouring to just fall off of you. One by one, let them fall to the ground.

You approach the golden sun that hangs so graciously high up in the sky, taking up all the space it needs, and you pause for a moment to simply bathe in its light. Feeling the deep warmth radiate on your skin, feeling the golden light washing over you, take a few deep breaths as you breathe in the golden light.

Surrounded by this bright, golden light, you are being called to remember yours, for the sun helps us to reveal our light and our shadows. What light are you being asked to reveal? What part of you is ready to express, shine and be seen?

Trust anything that rises; it may be your physical self or something you've created.

What are you ready to shine out to the world, and what may you need to let go of in order to shine as brightly as the sun?

Trust in whatever rises as you receive the messages from the sun, and allow them to absorb and seal into you.

When you are ready, it's time to return, back through the sunflower field, acknowledging and celebrating each sunflower and watching as, in return, they see and acknowledge you too.

SHARING PROMPTS

Begin to lead the sharing circle by asking a few questions and creating space for each Woman to write down what comes to her:

+ What insecurities are blocking you from shining your light?

✦ What might you have to let go of in order to shine?

✦ What are you being called to radiate to the world?

Once you feel called to open the sharing circle, invite each Woman to share something that came through in her journey and her responses to the sharing prompts.

ORACLE CARDS

Shuffle the deck then pass the cards around, inviting each Woman to connect to the spirit of the sun in Leo. Each Woman should set the intention to receive some deeper guidance and wisdom as they connect to its energy.

✦ Where am I being called to step deeper into my light?

✦ What is getting in way of me shining my light?

Share the cards you received and the message you felt the card gave you with the group.

RITUAL

Encourage each Woman to connect to the light they have remembered in this Circle, and to write down how they're being called to shine it in their own life. Hand out the craft tags, and have each Woman write their intentions onto theirs.

Then, one by one, invite each Woman to rise and walk around the sunflower circle three times, meditating on how and where they are being called to shine.

After the third cycle around, each Woman can select a sunflower from the centre and tie their craft tag to the stem as they raise the sunflower up into the sky, signalling they are ready to shine.

CLOSE THE CIRCLE

When everyone has selected their sunflower, return the energy back to the Circle. Invite each Woman to close their eyes, to recollect back to the light within them, to honour themselves for all the ways they are being called to spread their light, sending gratitude to all the Women who gathered beside them and honouring the energy of Leo for reminding them how to shine.

POST-CIRCLE

Encourage the Women to take their sunflower home with them, ready to serve as a reminder, all month, of their own light.

VIRGO CIRCLE

Be your own medicine

22 August – 23 September

WHO

Three or more Women

GATHER

+ ritual basket
+ 1 × bunch of foraged or store-bought herbs that you can make tea with (such as sage, mint, rosemary, thyme). Make sure you have enough sprigs for each Woman
+ 1 × bunch of wheat
+ hot water
+ 1 × teapot

Invite each Woman to bring their favourite mug with them.

ALTAR

Lay down your ritual cloth and place your pillar candle in the centre.
Create a flower circle using the herbs and wheat you gathered.
Place your teapot and ritual basket close by.

OPEN THE SPACE

Introduce yourself, the practice of the Women's Circle and the intention behind why you are gathering. Smudge the Women clockwise, then yourself, and then finally the altar space. Invite each Woman to introduce themselves and their astrology sign, and to share why they felt the calling to gather and what they are needing right at this moment.

ENERGY TALK

Virgo reminds us of our eternal purpose: to be of service. Its practical energy leads us towards the very basic acts of getting things done, working together and creating for the whole. As such, this is a beautiful time to harvest all the medicine and teachings that we've cultivated within us in order to share them with the world. This is a time of gathering and tending to ourselves in order to show up for the whole.

MEDITATION

Invite the Circle to take three deep breaths, in through the nose and out through mouth. Ask that they begin their journey by visualising themselves stepping out into a woodland.

The sun is setting, leaving a beautiful glow on the herbs and fruits that are ready to be harvested. You begin to observe what is there, what has borne fruit, what is ready for you to eat, and store. Pay attention. It doesn't need to make sense, just trust what you are being called to gather from this woodland.

Visualise yourself placing these objects into a wicker basket as you journey deeper and deeper into the forest. You see a deer in the distance. This beautiful deer begins to approach you from the woodland. Its gentle, dappled energy graces you.

The deer is here to remind you of how you have grown this year, and that you have fruits and herbs ready to be harvested and shared with the world.

The deer asks you what have you learnt this year. Perhaps you have learnt new skills, teachings or practices? Perhaps a bad experience taught you something, or a good experience gave you something? What qualities have you been asked to cultivate this year? Where have you softened? What fruits are living within you and how can you offer these to the people in your life? Where can you be of service?

Trust anything that rises in this moment. The deer comes to remind you that you don't need to wait until you're healed to help heal others; the gifts that live within you are enough, and will help to heal the world. Receiving that message, you begin to visualise the fruits within you, and place them in your wicker basket as you prepare to journey back to your sacred space with lots of medicine to give.

SHARING PROMPTS

Begin to lead the sharing circle by asking a few questions and creating space for each Woman to write down what comes to her:

✦ How are you being asked to be of service to the world?

+ What medicine have you returned back with?
+ How are you being shown you can serve your others?

Once you feel called to open the sharing circle, invite each Woman to share something that came through in her journey and her responses to the sharing prompts.

ORACLE CARDS

Shuffle the deck then pass the cards around, inviting each Woman to connect to the spirit of the sun in Virgo. Each Woman should set the intention to receive some deeper guidance and wisdom as they connect to its energy.

+ What else do you need to know about your medicine?
+ What is blocking you from receiving your medicine?

Guide the Women to share the cards they received and the message they felt their card gave them.

RITUAL

Invite each Woman to write down on a piece of paper the medicine that has come through for them, and how they're going to use it to be of service to the world.

One by one, inviting the Women to rise with their mug, welcome them to step over to the altar space and select a herb from the basket.

Holding the herb up to their heartspace, they then place it in their mug, intentionally pouring hot water from the teapot into their mug.

Stepping back to their seat, holding their brew in their hands, they continue to let their medicine seep in.

When everyone has brewed their tea, you can raise your cups up to the sky and sip your tea together.

CLOSE THE CIRCLE

Invite the Women to close their eyes, to reconnect back to the wisdom that the Circle has given them. Taking a moment to honour themselves for going on this journey, sending gratitude to all the Women who gathered beside them and honouring the energy of Virgo for reminding them of the medicine they hold.

POST-CIRCLE

Invite the Women to save the sprigs in their cup and use them throughout the month in a tea or a bath, or to make a tonic from them. Let the herbs serve as a reminder to nourish and tend to your inner world by remembering how you're being called to serve the outer world.

LIBRA CIRCLE

Return to the balance within

23 September – 22 October

WHO

Three or more Women

GATHER

- ✦ ritual basket
- ✦ 1 × large rose quartz
- ✦ 6 × smaller clear quartz
- ✦ 1 × bunch of pastel-coloured flowers

ALTAR

Lay down your ritual cloth and create a crystal grid, placing the large rose quartz in the centre and the smaller clear quartz around it, creating a circle. Place the petals and leaves from the flowers in and around the circle. Keep your ritual basket close by.

OPEN THE SPACE

Introduce yourself, the practice of the Women's Circle and the intention behind why you are gathering. Smudge the Women clockwise, then yourself, and then finally the altar space. Invite each Woman to introduce themselves and their astrology sign, and to share why they felt the calling to gather and where they currently feel out of balance in their lives.

ENERGY TALK

As we step into Libra, we are almost dancing into a new field of consciousness. But before we are able to fully immerse ourselves in it, we are given the opportunity with Libra to check in and rebalance our own energy. Libra is light and graceful, feminine and fluid. It beckons us to weigh up where we are living out of balance in our lives, so that we can return back to our wholeness.

MEDITATION

Invite the Circle to take three deep breaths in through the nose, and out through the mouth.

It's time to journey. Invite them to begin to visualise stepping out into a sunset sky, visualising all the beautiful pastel colours you see as day begins to turn to night. Blues and lilacs, pinks and oranges, taking in all the ethereal colours as you travel through them and journey further up into the clouds.

As you arrive, you are greeted by beautiful white fluffy clouds, soft enough to lie on.

Take some time to just lie on the clouds, noticing if you feel heavy or light. Tune into your energy. What have you been carrying heavy on your shoulders? What, if anything, has been weighing you down? How can you lighten the load? Where might you find harmony and balance within? Trust anything that rises as you notice where you are being called to balance the weight within.

In the safety of this sacred space, allow yourself to do whatever you need to do in order to balance your energy right now. If you need to cry, visualise yourself crying. If you need to let out rage or anger, visualise yourself screaming, or resting if you need to rest, or dancing if you need to move, or singing if you need to speak your truth. Whatever it is you need to do to balance out your energy, give it to yourself in this moment. Again, just trust whatever rises.

Notice how it feels to exist in space, giving yourself all that you need to come into truth and balance. Do you feel lighter? Do you feel more aligned?

When you're ready, I invite you to journey back to the space, in your centre, your grace, your essence.

SHARING PROMPTS

Begin to lead the sharing circle by asking a few questions and creating space for each Woman to write down what comes to her:

+ Where are you out of alignment within yourself?
+ What is being called back into balance?
+ How can you return to your harmonious state?

101

Once you feel called to open the sharing circle, invite each Woman to share something that came through for them on their guided journeys, or their responses to the sharing prompts.

ORACLE CARDS

Shuffle the deck then pass the cards around, inviting each Woman to connect to the spirit of the sun in Libra. Each Woman should set the intention to receive some deeper guidance and wisdom as they connect to its energy.

+ Where am I out of balance in my life?
+ What's the best use of my energy in returning back to wholeness?

Guide the Women to share the cards they received and the message they felt their card gave them.

RITUAL

Give each Woman a piece of a paper and a pen, inviting them to write a love letter to themselves.

With intention, invite them to begin writing a letter stating what they need to give themselves in order to return back into balance, and to end the letter with some sweet words of love and praise for themselves.

One by one, invite each Woman to read their love letter out loud to the Circle, activating the energy of Libra by using their feminine voice to send out your love to themselves.

CLOSE THE CIRCLE

Invite the Women to close their eyes, to reconnect back to the wisdom that the Circle has given them, taking a moment to honour themselves for returning back into balance, sending gratitude to all the Women who gathered beside them and honouring the energy of Libra for reminding them of their wholeness.

POST-CIRCLE

Invite the Women to hang their letters up or keep them somewhere they can see them throughout the rest of the month as a reminder of the love that lives within them, the love that creates the balance.

SCORPIO CIRCLE

Journey towards your inner shadows

23 October – 23 November

WHO

Three or more Women

GATHER

+ ritual basket
+ 1 × bowl of charged water*
+ 3 × seasonal pumpkins
+ a selection of store-bought or foraged mushrooms

*Charge it with a crystal and whisper an intention into the bowl the night before

Invite each Woman to bring an offering for their ancestors, such as a flower, a herb, a stone, crystal or pebble.

ALTAR

Lay down your ritual cloth and place the charged bowl of water in the centre. Create a fire circle around it by placing tea lights in a circle and lighting them. Disperse the pumpkins and mushrooms around the tea lights, and place your ritual basket beside the altar space.

OPEN THE SPACE

Introduce yourself, the practice of the Women's Circle and the intention behind why you are gathering. Smudge the Women clockwise, then yourself, and then finally the altar space. Invite each Woman to introduce themselves and their astrology sign, to share why they felt the calling to gather, and to introduce the offering they brought for their ancestor. They can then place this on the altar space.

ENERGY TALK

Scorpio can be an uncomfortable time of the year if we don't take the time to understand what it's trying to teach us. As such, creating a Circle in the energy field of Scorpio creates the perfect opportunity to work with the darkness in order to receive its medicine. We will create a space that allows us to step between the realms of our egos and truly enter the depths within, allowing us to surrender to what Scorpio is asking for to transform. Let's step between the worlds, and see what we find.

MEDITATION

Invite the Circle to take three deep breaths, in through the nose and out through the mouth. Visualise stepping out into a misty forest. Everything is covered in a fog, and all you see is a faint outline of trees that make you feel safe enough to continue to step through.

What other outlines can you see? Can you use any of your other senses, like touch, smell or hearing to take in the landscape? Take some time to just explore this space, trusting whatever you see or hear or feel.

As you continue to explore this forest, you notice the mist starting to lift. A beautiful animal awaits you and greets you, as you stand before an ancient well. The animal beckons you down the well, inviting you to take one step at a time, until you arrive at the bottom.

Here you are met by a very special person, one of your ancestors. Trust whoever comes through; it might be someone you remember, or perhaps someone who you have never met. Take a moment to just take them in, breathe them in. You know this ancestor is here to support and guide you, and to bring you any messages from the other realms.

Is there anything you want to ask your ancestor? Any fears you need support with? Any guidance you need in your life right now? Share anything you feel with your ancestor and just listen to what they say. Perhaps they have something they want to share with you, or tell you. Perhaps they want to hug you or kiss you.

Allow the medicine of them to be with you. Your ancestor then guides you to the water from the well. You use this water to purify yourself. You can pour it on your head, anoint yourself, bathe or shower in it. Whatever feels right.

You take a few more moments to just soak in this healing moment, gathering any last messages before saying farewell to your ancestor and journeying with your animal back up the well, into the misty forest, where you begin your quest back into your physical body. Take a few moments to ground the journey into your physical self, and when you're ready, gently come back to the room and open your eyes.

SHARING PROMPTS

Begin to lead the sharing circle by asking a few questions and creating space for each Woman to write down what comes to her:

+ What advice did you seek out from your ancestor?
+ What fears or suppressed emotions are wanting to be seen at this moment?
+ What shadows are seeking to be revealed right now?

Once you feel called to, open the sharing circle, inviting each Woman to share something that came through for them on their guided journeys or their responses to the sharing prompts.

ORACLE CARDS

Shuffle the deck then pass the cards around, inviting each Woman to connect to the spirit of the sun in Scorpio. Each Woman should set the intention to receive some deeper guidance and wisdom as they connect to its energy.

+ What shadow within am I being called to see?
+ What part of me am I being called to accept so that I can heal?

Guide the Women to share the cards they received and the message they felt their card gave them.

RITUAL

Invite each Woman to write down what fears or suppressed emotions are being asked to be alchemised on a piece of paper.

One by one, invite each Woman to step up to the altar space with their paper, and to burn it using a tea light in the fire circle.

When the fire gets to the top of the paper, they can place it in the bowl of water and watch as it dissolves and turns to nothing. They then gather the offering they brought with them from the altar space and seal the message they received into it.

CLOSE THE CIRCLE

Invite the Women to close their eyes, to reconnect back to the wisdom that the Circle has given them, taking a moment to honour themselves and their ancestors for journeying into their darkness.

POST-CIRCLE

Invite the Women to keep the offering with them as a reminder that they are protected, guided and never alone.

SAGITTARIUS CIRCLE

Seek out your inner adventurer

23 November – 21 December

WHO

Three or more Women

GATHER

- ✦ ritual basket
- ✦ 1 × fire bowl
- ✦ logs and candles (you are trying to create the feeling of sitting around a fire pit. If you can hold this Circle outdoors by a fire pit, even better!)
- ✦ any other seasonal herbs or evergreens you find
- ✦ 1 × postcard (and a few extra in case someone forgets to bring one)

Invite each Woman to bring a postcard with them.

ALTAR

Lay down your ritual cloth and place the fire bowl in the centre, then fill it with logs and little candles.

Intentionally place any herbs or evergreens around the circle.

OPEN THE SPACE

Introduce yourself, the practice of the Women's Circle and the intention behind why you are gathering. Smudge the Women clockwise, then yourself, and then finally the altar space. Invite each Woman to introduce themselves and their astrology sign, and to share why they felt the calling to gather and

106

what postcard they brought with them. Invite them to place their postcards on the altar once they have introduced them.

ENERGY TALK

The energy of Sagittarius invokes the adventurer within us to come out. It calls us to expand our horizons, to seek out a new way. Creating a Women's Circle at this time will allow us to vision, dream and expand our minds further than ever before. It's the time to go on an adventure with your spirit. So let us gather as we create a portal of expansion, sit by the fire, share our dreams ... and go on a journey.

MEDITATION

Invite the Circle to take three deep inhalations, in through the nose and out through the mouth. We're going on a journey to expand our horizons. The sun is setting, and it feels as though you are at the edge of the world, taking a deep breath in as you watch the sun getting smaller and smaller, and the sky begin to change colour.

The night sky begins to rise. We are standing in a liminal space between day and night. Time is standing still, the opportunities are endless and expansive. In this very moment we can go, be and do anything we want to.

So take a deep breath and let's go travelling. Bring forward a place in your mind where you'd like to go to. This could be a foreign place, perhaps somewhere you haven't been to before, somewhere that's been calling you ... Visualise yourself journeying there.

When you arrive, take in the land, where you are, what you are doing, how it feels.

What do you want to do in this place? What's the nature like here? Pay attention to everything.

What new smells and sights do you gather from here? What are the people like?

Are there things to taste and eat? How does this place make you feel? What energy do the people hold? What colours are present? Become aware of everything, for everything holds meaning.

When we travel to new lands, we are also travelling to the parts in us that are asking to come alive. What do you feel this place is giving you? Perhaps you may feel called to ask this land what it wanted you to remember? What knowledge or wisdom has this place given to you? Take a few moments to just contemplate this.

As you prepare to leave, the land hands you a souvenir to remind you that this place lives inside of you too, and you can journey here anytime you choose.

Gently returning to your physical body, take three deep inhales and exhales as you land back in your seat, back in the room, and gently open your eyes.

SHARING PROMPTS

Begin to lead the sharing circle by asking a few questions and creating space for each Woman to write down what comes to her:

+ Where did you go in your journey?
+ What did you learn about in this foreign space?
+ Describe the land and all that you saw.
+ How did this place show you where you're being called to expand your horizons?

Once you feel everyone is ready, open up the sharing circle, inviting each Woman to share something that came through for them on their guided journey or their responses to the sharing prompts.

ORACLE CARDS

Shuffle the deck then pass the cards around, inviting each Woman to connect to the spirit of the sun in Sagittarius. Each Woman should set the intention to receive some deeper guidance and wisdom as they connect to its energy.

+ Is there anything else the universe would like you to know about how you are being called to expand your horizons?

Guide the Women to share the cards they received and the message they felt their card gave them.

RITUAL

Guide the Women to tune into all they are being called to activate within them. Have them write themselves a postcard from that place within, telling themselves what they need to know as the adventurer and explorer they are.

Encourage them to write down any other wisdom they've learnt in the Circle tonight, through the meditation, the sharing and the cards ... and then one by one, go around the Circle and share your journeys with each other. Share the wisdom, tell your stories.

CLOSE THE CIRCLE

Invite the Women to close their eyes, to reconnect back to the wisdom that the Circle has given them, taking a moment to honour themselves and their inner explorer for journeying to the foreign lands within. Send gratitude to all the Women who gathered beside them and the energy of Sagittarius for expanding their horizons.

POST-CIRCLE

Invite the Women to take their postcards and post it to themselves. That way they will receive it a few days later, letting it be a reminder of the journeys they are being asked to take within, and the wisdom that is calling them.

CAPRICORN CIRCLE

Set intentional and authentic new year's resolutions

21 December – 22 January

WHO

Three or more Women

GATHER

- ✦ ritual basket
- ✦ 1 cup of little stones to create a small stone circle
- ✦ 1 × ribbon per Woman (thick enough to write on)
- ✦ wooden sticks
- ✦ foraged evergreens
- ✦ find a tree close to your home, that you can journey to

ALTAR

Create a little stone circle using the stones you've gathered. Place the ribbons around the stones, along with any other seasonal offerings, such as wooden sticks or foraged evergreens. Keep the ritual basket beside the altar.

OPEN THE SPACE

Introduce yourself, the practice of the Women's Circle and the intention behind why you are gathering. Smudge the Women clockwise, then yourself, and then finally the altar space. Invite each Woman to introduce themselves and their astrology sign, to share why they felt the calling to gather, and state one thing they're grateful for during the past year.

ENERGY TALK

The earth is sleeping, the trees are bare, the work is being done deep within; and although we cannot see it, we must trust that all will rise again in its divine timing. Trusting the rhythms and flow of nature is what Capricorn asks of us. Connecting to all we want to grow and achieve, yet remembering that we don't need to push ourselves up the mountain to get there; one step at a time, Capricorn whispers. So it's time to gather, to connect to all that you are wishing to manifest, set some powerful intentions and go hug some trees. Gently as you go, sisters.

MEDITATION

Invite the Circle to take three deep inhalations, in through the nose and out through the mouth. Begin to visualise yourself journeying to the base of a mountain. You can barely see the top of it, as it is covered in thick fluffy clouds.

So you begin your ascent, moving one step at a time, and taking in all that you see around you. Where are you? What is the temperature like here? What plants, shrubs or trees greet you on your path? Are there any animals there? Any sounds? Take it all in, as you focus on the rise and fall of your breath.

Spiralling further up the mountain, you begin to break through the heavy fog of clouds and emerge on the other side, with the peak of the mountain in plain view. You continue to journey one step at a time, spiralling further up.

You finally arrive at the top, taking a moment to stare down, amazed by how far you've climbed, by how many steps you had to take to get there. As you take this moment to feel gratitude for the work you've done, take a seat on the top of the mountain and begin tuning into the year ahead.

What would you like to accomplish and achieve this year; something physical, emotional, mental or spiritual? What new year's intention would you like to set? Trust anything that rises ...

When it feels complete, visualise yourself placing this intention in your heart-space, trusting that you will get there, you will achieve it, one step at a time.

Taking a moment to thank the mountain for its medicine, you take a few more breaths, breathing in this mountain air, then begin your journey back, spiralling down the peak of the mountain until you arrive at the base. Gently begin to journey back into your physical body, and when you are ready, open your eyes.

SHARING PROMPTS

Begin to lead the sharing circle by asking a few questions and creating space for each Woman to write down what comes to her:

+ What are you wanting to accomplish and achieve this year?
+ What, if any fears, do you have around this manifesting?

Once you feel everyone is ready, open up the sharing circle, inviting each Woman to share something that came through for them on their guided journey or their responses to the sharing prompts.

ORACLE CARDS

Shuffle the deck then pass the cards around, inviting each Woman to connect to the spirit of the sun in Capricorn. Each Woman should set the intention to receive some deeper guidance and wisdom as they connect to its energy.

✦ What one step can you take towards my new year's intention?

Guide the Women to share the cards they received and the message they felt their card gave them.

RITUAL

Encourage each Woman to connect to their new year's intention. One by one, invite the Women to select a ribbon from the altar space, and write down their intentions onto it.

Once everyone has written their wishes, gather your sisters and lead them outside.

Take off your shoes, and feel the earth beneath your feet.

Find a tree that you can all circle around. Take turns to speak your new year's intentions out loud, as you hold your ribbons.

Speak them to the earth beneath you, the tree in front of you and the sky above you.

If this is a tree that you can go to regularly, then tie your ribbon to its branches. If not, then keep your ribbon with you.

When everyone has spoken their new year's intentions out to the earth, return back inside.

CLOSE THE CIRCLE

Invite the Women to close their eyes, to reconnect back to the wisdom that the Circle has given them, taking a moment to honour themselves for the journey they've been on, sending gratitude to all the Women who gathered beside them and honouring the energy of Capricorn for guiding them back to their deepest new year's intentions.

POST-CIRCLE

Invite the Women who didn't tie their ribbons to the tree to find one on their way home, one they feel called to that they can visit easily; to set their intentions and tie it to a branch.

AQUARIUS CIRCLE

Uncover your role, in being part of the whole

22 January – 19 February

WHO

Three or more Women

GATHER

- ✦ ritual basket
- ✦ find a cause you'd all like to connect to together; a movement or organisation that stirs something up within you. Gather any symbols or objects that represent this
- ✦ download a star app to your phone

ALTAR

Lay down your ritual cloth and place any symbols, objects or seasonal offerings from nature into the shape of a circle. Dot tea lights and candles around it.

OPEN THE SPACE

Introduce yourself, the practice of the Women's Circle and the intention behind why you are gathering. Smudge the Women clockwise, then yourself, and then finally the altar space. Invite each Woman to introduce themselves and their astrology sign, to share why they felt the calling to gather and why they connect to this cause.

ENERGY TALK

On the wings of Aquarius you will fly, able to vision up a whole new world, if you choose.

This energy holds a powerful frequency that allows us to question, challenge and rise beyond what we see in front of us. Tapping into this energy in a Women's Circle will create the space to not only change your own beliefs but to imagine a new reality, one that if we work together, we can all step into. This sign paves the way for a more progressive world, asking us to think about *we*, instead of just *me*. This Circle is about gathering for the good of all, to gather for a cause close to your heart, and come together to build a whole new world.

MEDITATION

Invite the Circle to take three deep inhalations, in through the nose and out through the mouth. It's time to journey to the stars. Feel yourself grounded in your home as you stare out the window into the deep night sky. The sky is vast, clear and open, and you notice a constellation of stars twinkling at you.

The more you stare into the stars, the more they call you. Visualise yourself as you step outside, staring up at them deeper and deeper. It's almost as if they are singing to you. You begin to feel your feet lifting off the earth as you start to fly towards them.

As you fly through the night sky, you feel a sense of deep expansion, freedom, liberation, feeling almost weightless.

You finally arrive at a cluster of stars, and are in awe of the dazzling light they shine. As you step towards them, you take in their glittering light, feeling it vibrate and pulse through every cell of your being. These stars are here to remind you of the gifts you hold within, the gifts that you can use to create change. Spend a few moments breathing in their light, and inviting the stardust to guide you to the gifts and light within.

Knowing that you are made up of the exact same thing they are, the stars offer you some stardust to carry home with you in your pocket. The stardust is here to remind you of all the gifts and light you carry, of all the ways that you can light the way for others, and of all the ways you are here to remind others of their light, too.

It's time to journey back through the expansive night sky, feeling yourself flying through the night before landing safely, feeling the ground beneath your feet. As you feel yourself journeying back into your physical body, back into the Circle, gently open your eyes.

SHARING PROMPTS

Begin to lead the sharing circle by asking a few questions and creating space for each Woman to write down what comes to her:

+ What skill or gift do you hold within that you can offer the world?
+ What beliefs do you need to let go of in order to make a change?
+ What is one thing you can do this month to activate this change?

Once you feel everyone is ready, open up the sharing circle, inviting each Woman to share something that came through for them on their guided journey or their responses to the sharing prompts.

ORACLE CARDS

Shuffle the deck then pass the cards around, inviting each Woman to connect to the spirit of the sun in Aquarius. Each Woman should set the intention to receive some deeper guidance and wisdom as they connect to its energy.

+ What is the best use of my energy in supporting this cause?

Guide the Women to share the cards they received and the message they felt their card gave them.

RITUAL

Pass around some paper and pens as you create a plan of action with your sisters. This could be creating a fundraiser, volunteering, planning a march, creating a social media awareness campaign, holding an event, creating a short movie ... whatever you feel called towards.

Dedicate roles, responsibilities and jobs for each Woman to determine what you are going to do to support this cause. Take your time, and once this feels complete, gather your plan and head outside.

Find a spot under the dark night sky and sit under the cosmos. Spend a few moments you're your eyes closed, connecting to all that is, to all that you are, to all that you hold within you, remembering you are made of the same dust as the earth, the same light as the stars.

Tuning into the gifts you have been given and the action you've chosen to take, invite each Woman to find a star in the night sky. Once they've chosen their star, invite them one by one to rise and speak their action to the cosmos above.

CLOSE THE CIRCLE

Return indoors and invite the Women to close their eyes, to reconnect back to the wisdom that the Circle has given them, taking a moment to honour themselves for the journey they've been on, sending gratitude to all the Women who gathered beside them and honouring the energy of Aquarius for igniting the power within them to change the world.

POST-CIRCLE

If you have a star app you can find out what star it is that you wished upon, and every night you can send your intentions up to it.

114

PISCES CIRCLE

Embody and step into your highest self

19 February – 20 March

WHO

Three or more Women

GATHER

+ ritual basket
+ 1 × bowl of filtered/holy water – charge it with the intention of the space the night before
+ 1 × pack of watercolour paints per Woman
+ 1 × thin paintbrush per Woman
+ 1 × sheet of watercolour paper per Woman
+ 1 × water cup per Woman

ALTAR

Lay down your ritual cloth and place the charged bowl of water in the centre of the altar space. Keep your ritual basket close, along with the paints, paintbrushes, watercolour paper and water cups.

OPEN THE SPACE

Introduce yourself, the practice of the Women's Circle and the intention behind why you are gathering. Smudge the Women clockwise, then yourself, and then finally the altar space. Invite each Woman to introduce themselves and their astrology sign, and to share why they felt the calling to gather and how they're feeling at this moment.

ENERGY TALK

The oldest energy of all the signs, Pisces holds the key to your spirit.
All the signs have prepared us to step into this energy, where we can dive
into our deepest spiritual nature and float amid the divine. This is an artistic
and creative energy, so use this time to reconnect to your spiritual, sensitive,
psychic and intuitive gifts, and journey to remember all in life is not what it
seems; you are a spirit having a human experience.

MEDITATION

Invite the Circle to take three deep inhalations, in through the nose
and out through the mouth. Journeying into your body, as you begin to
scan your inner world from the crown of your head all the way down to
the feet, allow your breath to bring presence and awareness to your entire
physical being.

Once you've scanned your whole being, ask to be guided to a sacred space
within you. Take a deep breath, and trust the first place within you that you're
guided to. Once you feel it, travel there. As you step in, you enter the most
magikal sacred space of all – your dream space. Take it all in. Where are
you? What does it look like here? What surrounds you, What do you see?
What do you smell? How does it feel to be here? Spend some time exploring.

Out of the corner of your eye, you see a Woman emerging. Her silhouette
looks just like you, but she is surrounded by the purest bright white light.
She gets closer and closer, until you realise she is your higher self.

What does she look like?. Is she in human form, or does she look like a goddess,
an angel or mythic? What is she wearing? How does she smell? What energy is
she giving off? How does she make you feel when you're in her presence?

Take her in, breathe her in, your highest self. As you spend these moments
just existing in her presence, it's your opportunity to ask her anything.
What would you like to ask your highest self? Or perhaps you want to listen
out for a message she may hold for you? Spend this time together, being with
one another, as you allow yourself to remember all the answers you hold,
the wisdom you have and the truth of who you really are.

When you feel you've received all that you needed, thank your highest self.
Give her a hug and as you do, feel your two selves uniting – your physical and
your spiritual. Taking a deep breath, feel yourself stepping out of the sacred
space within you, knowing that it and she is there any time you need.

Slowly, feel yourself arriving back in your body. When you're ready, very gently
flutter your eyes open as you return back to the space.

SHARING PROMPTS

Begin the sharing circle by asking a few questions and creating space for each Woman to write down what comes to her:

+ Who is your highest spirit self, What does she look like?
+ What type of energy does she hold?
+ What messages did she hold for you?

Once you feel everyone is ready, open up the sharing circle, inviting each Woman to share something that came through for them on their guided journey or their responses to the sharing prompts.

ORACLE CARDS

Shuffle the deck then pass the cards around, inviting each Woman to connect to the spirit of the sun in Pisces. Each Woman should set the intention to receive some deeper guidance and wisdom as they connect to its energy.

+ What else does my highest self want me to know and remember?

Share the card you received and the message you felt the card gave you with the group.

RITUAL

Invite each Woman to call their highest self into their mind's eye as you pass around the watercolour paper, paints, brushes and cups.

One by one, ask each Woman to step towards the altar with her cup, and collect some water from the bowl in the centre. As they do, they can whisper into the water that they'd like to invoke their spirit into the art.

Tuning into the energy of her highest self, begin to paint a self-portrait using the watercolours.

Once you've finished your soul portraits, one by one, share them with the Circle, naming the qualities and any messages that wanted to come through.

CLOSE THE CIRCLE

Invite the Women to close their eyes, to reconnect back to the wisdom that the Circle has given them, taking a moment to honour themselves for the journey they've been on to connect to their highest self, sending gratitude to all the Women who gathered beside them and the energy of Pisces for guiding them back to their spirit.

POST-CIRCLE

Encourage each Woman to place their piece of art in a sacred space in their home; during the month go and sit with her, as time to remember your spirit within.

SEASONS

AS THE SEASONS CHANGE, SO DO WE ...

Honouring the changing of the seasons is a beautiful way to mark not only nature's transitions, but also the transitions that are happening within us.

This chapter will be an ode to reconnecting with the seasons, and how we can weave these ancient rituals into our lives.

Our ancient ancestors would have honoured the changing of the seasons with ritual and celebration. We don't have to dig too deep to see the resonance of these practices still present in our modern lives.

Consider Christmas, Easter and Halloween. When stripped back, all these celebrations would reveal deep rituals of reverence, connection and acknowledgement of the land and how nature was changing.

The wheel of the year is typically connected with Celtic and Pagan traditions. However, we all walk the same year, and similar festivities can be found across many ancient religions and cultures. In most religions, the main festivals are all embedded with the same intentions. No matter how different we may seem, we all walk the same earth. When we peel back our different practices, we can see the oneness shining through.

We can look to ancient cultures for inspiration as to how we can honour the changing of the seasons. We do this in the hope that we can learn to live in harmony, deep communion and connection with nature once again.

For the sake of this book, we will divide the wheel of the year into the four widely known seasons of spring, summer, autumn and winter.

Each season holds its own medicine, teachings and gifts that are ours to explore, receive and acknowledge.

The seasons remind us of just how slowly nature changes. Every three months or so we step into a new cycle, a new season. The seasons remind us to take life slow, a beautiful remedy to the fast-paced lifestyle we've found ourselves in. Let the seasons remind you to be intentional, knowing and trusting that everything has its place and time, and every season is crucial to the whole.

Let us begin to walk through the wheel of the year step by step, together.

SPRING EQUINOX CIRCLE

Connect to the spring equinox

Sunrise on the morning of the spring equinox, if possible

✳   ✳   ✳

WHO

Three or more Women who are seeking to gather to set some powerful intentions

GATHER

Somewhere in nature, where the energy of spring is present. This can be a beautiful bluebell meadow or your garden, and indoors is totally fine if you can't make it outside.

+ ritual basket
+ 4 × bunches of seasonal flowers such as wild garlic, daffodils, crocuses, bluebells
+ 1 × roll of natural twine
+ 1 × scissors
+ 1 × craft tag per Woman

Invite Women to forage at least three seasonal flowers or herbs. Remind them to pick with intention and gratitude.

ALTAR

Lay down your ritual cloth and create a flower circle using the seasonal flowers you've gathered. Place your pillar candle in the centre, and your ritual basket holding your twine, scissors and smudge beside it. Invite each Woman to place their offerings in the middle of the altar space in the centre of the circle.

OPEN THE SPACE

Introduce yourself, the practice of the Women's Circle and the intention behind why you are gathering. Smudge the Women clockwise, then yourself, and then finally the altar space. Invite each Woman to introduce themselves and their astrology sign, and to share why they felt the calling to gather and what this shift in season is bringing up for them.

ENERGY TALK

The spring equinox marks the beginning of spring. It's a moment when we can pause before stepping into a new phase in our lives.

It has been seen by many ancient cultures as the start of the new year, where the wheel begins again. This time was once seen as an opening, a portal through which we could connect and commune with nature, spirits and the universe before stepping into the new season ahead.

As such, this is a powerful time to gather with Women and to re-enact the celebrations, festivities and rituals of more nature-based living.

The equinox translates to equal day and night. The light and darkness are in balance, and thus this becomes a powerful indicator to ensure that the light and dark within us are in balance too.

The equinoxes are not just a beautiful way to acknowledge and give gratitude for all that is happening in nature outside of us, but just as importantly, they are an opportunity to acknowledge what may be happening or being asked inside of us.

MEDITATION

Invite the Circle to take three deep inhalations, in through the nose and out through the mouth. Invite them to ground into the earth beneath them as they settle into this sacred space.

Become aware of your breath, become present to it, witnessing its ebb and flow. The more present you become to what's happening inside of you, the more we can bring our presence to all that is happening outside of us too.

For we are standing on the edge of the moment where winter has become spring, where the seasons have changed, and where the seeds of potential are being sown.

So take a moment to listen, to pay attention, to connect, to witness what is going on inside of you.

Breathe it all in, knowing there is no judgement needed, just a gentle awareness (Pause for at least one minute here.)

Now take a moment to give thanks to winter, to all the darkness that has been, to the colder months, to the chilling air, to the work that has been going on deep within ... as we gently prepare to welcome spring.

When you're ready, in your own time, feel the weight of your body on your seat as you gently wiggle your fingers and toes and open your eyes.

SHARING PROMPTS

Begin to lead the sharing circle by asking a few questions and creating space for each Woman to write down what comes to her:

+ Where are you in and out of balance in your life?
+ How are you being called to honour both the light and the dark within?
+ What seeds are you being called to plant?
+ What are you wishing to become fertile this spring?

Once you feel everyone is ready, open up the sharing circle, inviting each Woman to share something that came through for them on their guided journey or their responses to the sharing prompts.

ORACLE CARDS

Shuffle the deck then pass the cards around, inviting each Woman to connect to the spirit of the spring equinox. Each Woman should set the intention to receive some deeper guidance and wisdom as they connect to its energy.

+ What am I being called to plant this spring?
+ What is stopping my seeds growing?

Guide the Women to share the cards they received and the message they felt their card gave them.

RITUAL

Encourage the Women to tune into all that they're ready to plant this spring, then to write down an intention on a craft tag and tie it to a long piece of string.

Invite each Woman to gather the herbs and flowers they foraged.

Using the intention string, invite them one-by-one to begin to weave together their medicine bundle, almost as if they were crafting a bouquet of flowers. (It may serve you to demonstrate first.) Ensure they tie and wrap the bundle together with their intention in their mind's eye.

CLOSE THE CIRCLE

Invite the Women to close their eyes, to reconnect back to the wisdom that the Circle has given them, taking a moment to honour themselves for the journey they've been on to connect to the seeds' longing to be planted, and to send gratitude to all the Women who gathered beside them and to the energy of the spring equinox for guiding them back to their spirit.

POST-CIRCLE

Invite each Woman to keep their bundles in a safe space and to hold them, smell them and connect to them throughout the season, in order to remember all that they are ready to plant.

SUMMER SOLSTICE CIRCLE

A Circle to celebrate the summer solstice

On the evening of the summer solstice

*   *   *

WHO

Three or more Women who are seeking to gather to honour the longest day of the year

GATHER

A park, garden, beach (weather permitting). Somewhere in nature.
As it is the longest day of the year, hold a Circle in the evening, while it's still light outside, and celebrate with a picnic.

- ✦ ritual basket
- ✦ 1 × bunch of sunflowers
- ✦ 1 × bunch of any other seasonal flowers
- ✦ 1 × floral wire and tape (enough for the circumference of each Woman's head)
- ✦ 1 × wire scissors
- ✦ food and crockery for picnic

Invite the Women to forage some seasonal flowers to bring with them to the Circle, as well as a dish to share, and a blanket to sit on.

ALTAR

Lay down your ritual cloth and create a flower circle using the heads of the sunflowers. In the middle, place candles, crystals and anything else you feel called to.

OPEN THE SPACE

Introduce yourself, the practice of the Women's Circle and the intention for gathering. Smudge the Women clockwise, then yourself, and then finally the altar space. Invite each Woman to introduce themselves and their astrology sign, and to share why they felt the calling to gather and what this shift in season is bringing up for them.

ENERGY TALK

The sun has reached its peak and hangs high in the sky. At this moment, we welcome the longest day of the year, the marker that we have shifted from the waxing/rising energy of spring into the full bloom of summer as we step into the next season and cycle of summer.

The land is abundant, filled with flowers, herbs, plants. Everything has bloomed around us, and the sun is shining down on it all. It is a time to bask, honour and give deep gratitude for all the light that has shone down on us, for all that the sun has charged within us, and for all the life, growth and bounty it has bestowed. On the summer solstice we are given a beautiful opportunity to pause, reflect, celebrate and acknowledge the light of the sun.

People have been gathering to honour the solstice and the changing of the seasons since the beginning of time. We see this when we look at the ancient stone circles that were all positioned intentionally to welcome the sun on this powerful day – the Temple of the Sun in Peru, Stonehenge in England, the Ring of Brodgar in Scotland, the Pyramids in Egypt, to name just a few.

The solstice offers us an invitation to connect to this powerful ritual once again, to honour the sun and to bask in the glory of the light. Cultures from around the world celebrate the solstice with celebration, music, dance and joy – this is probably where the idea of summer festivals stemmed from. During the summer months, we all seek a space to gather together, to celebrate all that has been, as we can finally exhale and just enjoy.

MEDITATION

Invite the Circle to take three deep inhalations, in through the nose and out through the mouth, then gently welcome your natural rhythm of breathing back.

Become aware of your breath, become present to it, witnessing the ebb and flow. The more present you become to what's happening inside of you, the more you can bring your presence to all that is happening outside of you too.

For the seeds we planted are beginning to bloom, and we are given a moment in time to sit back and reflect on all the ways we have grown.

What have you created for yourself this year? No matter how big or small, allow yourself to receive the glory of you.

The fruits of your labour, the gifts you've manifested.

Trust whatever rises to the surface, and allow yourself to witness, reflect and receive the light of all that you are.

(Pause for at least one minute.)

Bring this light back into the room, as you very gently feel yourself returning back to your seat, wiggling your fingers and toes, and opening your eyes.

SHARING PROMPTS

Begin to lead the sharing circle by asking a few questions and creating space for each Woman to write down what comes to her:

+ What are you proud of?
+ What are you grateful for?
+ What blessings are in your life?
+ What can you give to others?

Once you feel everyone is ready, open up the sharing circle, inviting each Woman to share something that came through for them on their guided journey or their responses to the sharing prompts.

ORACLE CARDS

Shuffle the deck then pass the cards around, inviting each Woman to connect to the spirit of the summer solstice. Each Woman should set the intention to receive some deeper guidance and wisdom as they connect to its energy.

+ How am I being called to see my light within?
+ What do I need to let go of I order to see my light?

Share what message you received with the Circle, and how you feel it connects to what you have uncovered in the space so far.

Invite all the Women to gather the flowers they foraged and any flowers they feel called to gather from the Circle.

Demonstrate how to make a flower crown.

Calling in the glory of yourself, and holding the vibration of all the light you are being asked to witness in yourself, begin to gather the wire, perhaps asking the Woman beside you to help cut the perfect sized wire for your head.

Once you have your wire, you will want to start weaving your flowers onto it, taping the stems down.

Ensure you place each flower down with intention.

Keep going around and around until the crown is full of flowers.

Then, one by one, holding up your flower crowns, place them on top of your head, and invite the other Women to witness you as you each place your crowns on your head like the queens that you are!

CLOSE THE CIRCLE

Invite the Women to close their eyes, to reconnect back to the wisdom that the Circle has given them, taking a moment to honour themselves for the journey they've been on to connect to the seeds longing to be planted, and to send gratitude to all the Women who gathered beside them and to the energy of the summer solstice for guiding you back to your spirit.

POST CIRCLE

Once you have closed your Circle, it's time to feast! Bring forward all your food, have a picnic, light a bonfire if you feel called to, and stay up all night radiating, laughing, singing and dancing in the joy of summer, in the joy of you!

AUTUMN EQUINOX CIRCLE

A gathering to honour the autumn equinox

The weekend of autumn equinox

✳   ✳   ✳

WHO

Three or more Women

GATHER

Somewhere quiet in nature, such as a woodland, a meadow, a back garden or quiet area of a park. You want to go somewhere that has access to wild grown plants, herbs or flowers.

+ ritual basket
+ 6 × apples
+ 1 × bunch of wheat
+ any other seasonal herbs or flowers you feel called to bring
+ anything else that symbolises the harvest of autumn
+ 1 × large roll of string

Invite the Women to bring a basket, a pair of scissors, and a blanket to sit on.

ALTAR

Create your sacred space in nature. Lay down your ritual cloth, and on top of it create your flower circle, using the apples, wheat and any other seasonal herbs and flowers you feel called to bring. Light a candle in the centre, and sprinkle some tea lights, crystals or any other symbols within the spaces of the circle. Place your ritual basket beside it.

OPEN THE SPACE

Introduce yourself, the practice of the Women's Circle and the intention behind why you are gathering. Smudge the Women clockwise, then yourself, and then finally the altar space. Invite each Woman to introduce themselves and their astrology sign, and to share why they felt the calling to gather and what this shift in season is bringing up for them.

ENERGY TALK

As we reach the autumn equinox, we return back to the balance of light and day that we experienced in spring. Six months on, we are given another opportunity in our year to return inwards. This is a time when we can pause, recalibrate and reconnect to our energy.

Yet this time, we prepare for the descent into the darkness. The nights grow longer, the days are shorter, the air is chillier, the trees return their sap to the ground, and we watch as nature turns from a vibrant lush green to more muted yellows and oranges. The trees have borne their fruit, and so have we. It's time to stop, and to reap what we have sown.

MEDITATION

Invite the Circle to take three deep inhalations, in through the nose and out through the mouth, then gently welcome your natural rhythm of breathing back.

Become aware of your breath, become present to it; witnessing its ebb and flow. The more present you become to what's happening inside of you, the more we can bring our presence to all that is happening outside of us too.

As the wheel of the year turns, and we prepare to enter these darker months, it's time to harvest all that we have grown. To turn our fruits into our medicine, to gather the light within us, and to let it be the light we return to as we descend into the darkness.

Tune into all that you have grown, to all the challenges and obstacles you've faced along the way, to all the teachings and wisdom it has brought you and to all the lessons learnt.

Harvest everything you need to remember your power, your strength, your light.

(Pause for at least one minute.)

When you're ready, feel yourself arriving back in the space, returning back with all that you need, as you gently wiggle your fingers and toes, and open your eyes.

SHARING PROMPTS

Begin to lead the sharing circle by asking a few questions and creating space for each Woman to write down what comes to her:

✦ What wisdom have you been asked to gather?
✦ What medicine lives within you?
✦ What fruits of our labour are you harvesting?
✦ What do you need to gather for our inner selves?

Once you feel everyone is ready, open up the sharing circle, inviting each Woman to share something that came through for them on their guided journey or their responses to the sharing prompts.

ORACLE CARDS

Shuffle the deck then pass the cards around, inviting each Woman to connect to the spirit of the autumn equinox. Each Woman should set the intention to receive some deeper guidance and wisdom as they connect to its energy.

✦ What might you need to remember to support you on your journey into the darker months?

Guide the Women to share the cards they received and the message they felt their card gave them.

RITUAL

Tune into your intentions and invite the Women to go off and explore the natural surroundings. Invite nature to guide you, be led by the flowers and herbs that call you. What's getting your attention? What do you stumble upon?

Trusting your intuition, gather and harvest only what you need, making sure to leave enough for others seeking to harvest too.

Once you've gathered your collection of herbs and flowers, return back to the Circle and sit with your bundle for a while, feeling the energy of the leaves, the petals, the smells.

Take some string and begin to create your very own medicine bundle.

You can begin to seal your energy into your gathered collection, perhaps sealing any intentions, wishes or prayers into them.

Then you will wait to activate this energy, by rising one by one, holding all that you've harvested, and naming your wishes out into the ether.

CLOSE THE CIRCLE

Invite the Women to close their eyes, to reconnect back to the wisdom that the Circle has given them. Encourage all present to take a moment to honour themselves for all that they've harvested, and to send gratitude to all the Women who gathered beside them in the Circle and to the energy of the autumn equinox for allowing them to reflect on this time.

POST-CIRCLE

Encourage the Women to keep their medicine bundles somewhere sacred at home. Perhaps they may be called to sprinkle a herb in their bath one day, or to make a tea, a tincture or a flower water out of them, to remind them of all the medicine that they hold to support themselves.

WINTER SOLSTICE CIRCLE

A Circle to honour the winter solstice

The evening of the winter solstice

*　　　*　　　*

WHO

Three or more Women who are called to honour the darkest day of the year

GATHER

Forest, woodland, park, somewhere with trees, at twilight, just before it gets fully dark.

- ✦ ritual basket
- ✦ 1 × bunch of eucalyptus
- ✦ 1 × bunch of evergreens (ivy, holly, etc.)
- ✦ 1 × bunch of foraged sticks
- ✦ 2–3 × ribbons per Woman gathering
- ✦ 1 × tea light per Woman gathering
- ✦ a collection of cosy blankets/sheepskins, etc.

Invite the Women to bring a lantern or torch, and an extra blanket to wrap around themselves.

ALTAR

Create a sacred space in nature, ensuring there are enough blankets for everyone. Place the candle in the centre, and create a flower circle using eucalyptus, evergreens and any sticks you find. Place tea lights in the spaces in between the circle.

OPEN THE SPACE

Introduce yourself, the practice of the Women's Circle and the intention behind why you are gathering. Smudge the Women clockwise, then yourself, and then finally the altar space. Invite each Woman to introduce themselves and their astrology sign, and to share why they felt the calling to gather and what this shift in season is bringing up for them.

ENERGY TALK

As the winter solstice arrives, we step into the longest night and darkest day of the year. We have entered the peak of darkness, and now we wait patiently for the wheel of the year to continue its journey back towards the light.

At this time we are once again offered a powerful moment to trust, to trust that the light will return, to allow ourselves to surrender into the darkness, and to remember that it is in the dark where everything is born.

And so we pause to question what medicine this time of year is offering us. Although we step into what feels like the depths of winter at this time, it is also a moment to remember that the light will soon return, for the darkest of days is actually the beginning of the return to the light.

We only have to look to nature to begin to understand what we're being asked. The trees are bare, yet so much is happening within their roots. Winter is a time of rest, of deep replenishment, a time to cultivate and light the fire within to keep you warm for the month ahead.

It may seem like nothing's moving, but all the work is happening within, so allow yourself to surrender to the energy of winter.

MEDITATION

Invite the Circle to take three deep inhalations, in through the nose and out through the mouth, then gently welcome your natural rhythm of breathing back.

Become aware of your breath, become present to it, witnessing its ebb and flow.

The more present you become to what's happening inside of you, the more we can bring our presence to all that is happening outside of us too.

We have now arrived at the darkest point of the year. The descent is over, and we will now slowly begin the gentle ascent back to the light.

How does it feel to step into the darkness? Where are you trying to resist the dark within yourself?

Can you find that strength within, knowing that seasons change, yet every season has its purpose? What is the darkness trying to show you right now? What are these emotions trying to bring forward within you?

How can you find gratitude for the dark, for all it has brought to you, for all the ways it's helping you grow?

(Pause for at least one minute.)

When you're ready, feel yourself arriving back in the space, returning back with all that you need, as you gently wiggle your fingers and toes, and open your eyes.

SHARING PROMPTS

Begin to lead the sharing circle by asking a few questions and creating space for each Woman to write down what comes to her:

+ How does it feel to be in the dark?
+ What do you feel you're being shown here?
+ Where can we bring gratitude for our experiences?

Once you feel everyone is ready, open up the sharing circle, inviting each Woman to share something that came through for them on their guided journey or their responses to the sharing prompts.

ORACLE CARDS

Shuffle the deck then pass the cards around, inviting each Woman to connect to the spirit of the winter solstice. Each Woman should set the intention to receive some deeper guidance and wisdom as they connect to its energy.

+ What do I need to bring a deeper sense of gratitude?
+ What lessons are trying to come through in the dark?
+ What is the best use of my energy during these winter months?

Guide the Women to share the cards they received and the message they felt their card gave them.

RITUAL

Encourage each Woman to tune into the messages and intentions they received from the Circle.

Give each Woman a few ribbons, and begin to walk through the trees, using this as a walking meditation. Encourage the Women to be open to any tree that calls them, and to tie their gratitude ribbons onto their branches, taking time to honour all the work this tree is doing within, as they honour all the work the Women are doing within too.

Give thanks to the tree, give the tree a hug if you feel called, or maybe even a kiss, and then return to the Circle with intention.

When everyone has arrived back, one by one, step up to the Circle and collect a tea light, igniting the flame using the candle in the middle of the circle. Take a moment as you hold the flame in the palms of your hand to speak your intention outwards, calling in and acknowledging the light within you.

CLOSE THE CIRCLE

Invite the Women to close their eyes, to reconnect back to the wisdom that the Circle has given them, taking a moment to honour themselves for all that they've found in the darkness, and to send gratitude to all the Women who gathered beside them in the Circle and to the energy of the winter solstice for allowing them to find the light in the dark.

POST-CIRCLE

It may be nice to visit your tree every so often, to tend to it, perhaps to tie some more ribbons, and give it a hug every now and then. I'm sure it would be so grateful for your return. As the days draw lighter and the light returns, you can walk with your tree, watching how she buds and blooms, acknowledging her journey alongside your own.

If you ever need to remember your light during the darker months, light your tea light as a reminder.

NURTURE

NEW BEGINNINGS • HONOURING ENDINGS
MANIFESTATION

NOW WE'VE EXPLORED the cyclical energy of nature and how we can weave that into our Circles, we now turn towards the more cyclical nature of our inner worlds. Life is always giving us moments to pause, reflect and acknowledge changes in our own lives, and just like the moon, the sun and the seasons, we too are constantly in ebb and flow.

I know in my life, there have been poignant moments where I have deeply sought out a community, a space to share my highs and lows in a more symbolic and meaningful way, so that I could be seen, witnessed and held as I moved through the cycles of my own life.

As a culture, we have forgotten what we can bring to one another in the times when we need support. Over the next few chapters we will be looking at moments where we can gather around each other, to support and hold space for one another, celebrate, grieve, acknowledge and honour the cycles of our own lives. We will be offering alternative ways we can gather, and ways we can be there for one another.

If you resonate with any of these Circles and are hearing the calling to have one held for you, my invitation would be to reach out to one of your girlfriends and share the work with her.

As you call her to hold this sacred space for you, you spread this work deeper; and when the time is right, I'm sure she will ask you to hold the space for her too.

I truly believe, as we journey through the cycles of our own lives, that we can give and receive such potent medicine simply by knowing how to support each other in the moments we need support.

NEW BEGINNINGS

AS ONE CYCLE ENDS, ANOTHER BEGINS.

In life, we are constantly mirroring that same life cycle that we see in the moon, the sun, the seasons.

I like this to be my reminder of how connected we are to nature. As we honour the new moon, the rebirth of spring, the awakening of new beginnings, we too can bring that into the moments in our lives that are presenting us with a fresh new start. This is an invitation to gather your sisters around you, to hold a Women's Circle, to create a sacred space when entering a new phase of your life; whether a new love, a new job, a new start. To honour life's precious invitation to begin again, and embrace all the opportunities that lie ahead of us at this time.

My wish is that these spaces become the norm, and that we remember that holding space, celebrating, and witnessing each other as we move through the new beginning in each of our lives is the best gift we can give.

NEW LOVE CIRCLE

To honour the start of a new relationship

During the honeymoon phase of a new relationship

*   *   *

WHO

Gather her closest girlfriends – think of the girls who've been there for her through thick and thin; her ride-or-die girls!

GATHER

- ✦ ritual basket
- ✦ 1 × big bunch of roses
- ✦ 5 × rose quartz

ALTAR

Lay down your ritual cloth. Place a candle in the middle, and create a rose quartz flower circle around the candle using petals, flower heads, leaves and rose quartz between them. Work intuitively to make an intentional mandala. Place the ritual basket beside the altar.

OPEN THE SPACE

Introduce yourself, the practice of the Women's Circle and the intention behind why you are gathering. Smudge the Women clockwise, then yourself, and then finally the altar space. Invite each Woman to introduce themselves and their astrology sign, and to share why they felt the calling to gather and why they chose to be here tonight.

ENERGY TALK

When we start a new relationship, most of us begin from a place of fear or unrealistic expectations; either you're knee-deep in the ecstasy of the honeymoon phase, or you're feeling the fears creep in and you find yourself sabotaging this new chapter.

The deepest lessons I've learnt in life have emerged through the romantic relationships I've had. As such, whether this new love is your forever person, or a teacher for you, you will not be able to receive the medicine of this new relationship if you are not open to it.

This Circle is about grounding. It's about coming back down to earth, to your body, to your heart so you can welcome this new chapter in your life, in your truth, and thus be open to all the magik that awaits you.

New relationships can bring up all sorts of old wounds, fears, projections and illusions, and so can create the most fertile opportunity for us to look at ourselves, to heal wounds and create a new outcome.

This Circle is not so much about celebrating a new love as it is about creating a safe and sacred space to honour this new beginning, to let go of anything coming up that may be sabotaging, and to truly welcome your heart to open so you can let this love in.

MEDITATION

Guide the Circle through a self-love meditation.

Invite the Circle to take three deep inhalations, in through the nose and out through the mouth, then guide them to breathe deeply into their hearts' spaces, again taking three deep breaths into the heart, and exhaling out from the heart.

Welcoming them to open their hearts to the Circle, ask that an intention rise up from within their heart today. How does their heart want them to feel?

Trusting the words they received, gently guide them back into their body and, when they're ready, to open their eyes.

SHARING PROMPTS

The sharing circle can create a powerful opportunity to get vulnerable, to have a space where the Woman who is honouring a new love can share, release and be open about anything that may be blocking them from fully receiving this new opportunity to let love in. This Circle is a coming home; a coming home back to your heart.

+ What do you feel you may be projecting already onto this relationship?
+ Do you have any expectations of what this relationship will be?
+ If you saw this relationship as a mirror, what is your new partner reflecting back to you?
+ What qualities do you love about your partner? Can you acknowledge those qualities in yourself?
+ What qualities are you triggered by? Can you acknowledge those qualities in yourself?
+ What may you need to let go of in order to come back to your heartspace?
+ What may you need to acknowledge, celebrate and reveal in yourself in order to show up in your fullest?
+ What can you do to show up authentically in this new relationship?
+ Do you feel you need to hide certain parts of yourself in order to feel enough?

Allow time to tune into these questions and to really create a safe space to let any answers come up, be witnessed and be heard, for this is where the healing happens.

ORACLE CARDS

Invite each Woman to pull a card with the intention of receiving information about what energy is needed to support her further in this new relationship.

+ What message does [name] need to know in order to support her in her new relationship?

Go around the Circle, each sharing the cards you received and what you feel the message is.

RITUAL

Invite the Woman you've gathered for to take a few moments to write down any wisdom, guidance or messages received in the Circle.

In doing this, she is connecting to what emerged, to what she is being asked to bring forward into this new chapter; this can be an intention, an action, or a new belief.

Invite her to take a few moments to write herself a love letter; a letter that declares all the beautiful qualities in her, all that she wishes to share with this new partner, and any fears she is ready to let go of. Begin the letter with *'Dear* [name]*'* and end it with *'Love from* [name]*'* ... this is a way to acknowledge and honour her higher self as she writes this letter.

With her letter, guide the Woman to step forward to the altar space, receive a rose quartz crystal from the centre, place it in the palm of her hand as she closes her eyes, as she seals her intention into the crystal.

This may be a lovely opportunity for her sisters to stand around her, and shower her with rose petals.

CLOSE THE CIRCLE

Once you have sealed all the energy you feel called to into the rose quartz crystal, you can close the Circle by inviting all the Women to close their eyes and to reflect upon the wisdom that the Circle has given them. For even if this Circle was in honour of [name], it was carrying important messages for everyone to receive. Take a moment for the Women to honour themselves for returning back to the Circle, to send gratitude to all the Women who gathered beside them in the Circle and to the energy of this new relationship ... let it be the start of something magikal.

POST-CIRCLE

Encourage the Woman to let her rose quartz be her ally, infused with the energy she wishes to bring into her new relationship. Tell her to keep it close and whenever she feels disconnected from her heartspace to reread her letter, or call up one of her sisters and let them mirror back what she may have forgotten.

HONOURING ENDINGS

THE MOMENTS IN OUR LIFE WHEN SOMEONE OR SOMETHING HAS BEEN TAKEN AWAY FROM US ARE OFTEN OUR DARKEST DAYS.

Yet endings are very much a part of the circle of life. They bring discomfort, resistance, pain and often struggle. Yet with that also comes deep medicine, wisdom and teachings.

For the truth is, there is nothing more nourishing than sharing your grief honestly and openly in a Circle with others who can witness your loss, without trying to make it better.

Together we hold space for grief to be welcomed in all its tender, raw and wild expressions.

Grief doesn't want to be fixed, advised or saved, it just wants to be seen, deeply witnessed and loved. When we sit in a Circle that honours endings, we are consciously embodying what it means to say, *'I am here for you'.*

Nothing is more nourishing for the grieving heart than a safe space to let grief be seen, released and witnessed. In this chapter, I will offer you three different Circles to honour a grieving heart. The Circles are centred around one individual, and the support from those who love them. However, you can also adapt each of these to hold a community Circle in which each person is invited to bring and share their own experience of loss.

GRIEF CIRCLE

A sacred space to offer support to a grieving sister

Whenever feels right for the bereaved person. Some people choose to hold space in the immediate aftermath of a loss, while for others it feels right to leave some time for the shock and numbness to reside. It can also be beautiful to hold a grief Circle around an anniversary or birthday.

*　　　*　　　*

There is perhaps no greater sense of ending than when we experience the deep, soul-shifting bereavement of losing a loved one. The ensuing grief changes the entire landscape of our lives, yet despite its universality, grief is largely unsupported and unspoken about.

I feel that there is a second, perhaps even more damaging grief that follows the death of a loved one, and that is the feelings of loneliness and isolation we can experience as we try to navigate loss without the spaces, rituals and elders to support us.

We were never meant to experience life's struggles alone. However, in our modern world we have lost sight of the inextricable link between love and loss. Like sisters, grief and gratitude go hand in hand, and both need to be given space to be seen.

With this in mind, I invite you to welcome grief, loss and sorrow into a sacred Circle and to recognise that life's endings require just as much attention as its beginnings. Thank you dear Nici Harrison, for gifting us this grief circle.

WHO

A group of supportive soul sisters

GATHER

+ ritual basket
+ 1 × bunch of flowers
+ 1 × jug of water
+ 1 × empty bowl

Invite the Women to bring a flower, stone or something else that feels supportive to the bereaved. Invite the bereaved to bring any images, objects or words that connect them to what/who they have lost.

ALTAR

Lay down your ritual cloth and create a flower circle with your flowers of choice. Fill the circle with images or objects that people have brought with them. Place all other items in the ritual basket, keeping it close by.

OPEN THE SPACE

Introduce yourself, the practice of the Women's Circle and the intention behind why you are gathering. Smudge the Women clockwise, then yourself, and then finally the altar space.Invite each Woman to introduce themselves, and to share why it was important that they chose to be here tonight.

ENERGY TALK

A grief circle is an intentional space for grief to be shared in all its magnitude and truth, to be deeply received and witnessed, and held in loving compassion. We gather together to hold space for our dear friend who is experiencing loss and grief. We sit with them in their sorrows, not trying to fix or change the experience, but walking alongside them. In this Circle, we offer a container in which their grief is given full permission to be expressed and seen. We are holding them like the banks of the river, and their grief is the flowing water. Your grief is welcome here.

MEDITATION

Invite the group to close their eyes and connect with how their body feels on the seat beneath them, bringing their full presence to the holding of the ground, and acknowledging the supportive energy of Mother Earth, who is always carrying us.

Thank the group for being here today, recognising that the greatest gift they can give to the person bereaved is to sit with them as they are navigating their loss. I invite you to bring three qualities into the Circle: presence, acceptance and compassion.

✦ We offer our deepest awareness, our capacity to sit here and witness grief as it ebbs and flows, as we hold space for grief to be just as it is.

✦ We meet grief with acceptance, letting go of judgement or expectations and allowing it to be as wild, vast and raging as it truly is, as we create the container for grief to move.

✦ We bring our boundless compassion and kindness, so that true alchemy can take place, transforming grief, giving it space to be seen and released.

With these three qualities of presence, acceptance and compassion, bring forward into your mind's eye the ways in which you can support your friend at this time. Let these intentions fill you as we hold space for our dear friend to grieve, acknowledging that grief is an ongoing journey, but one that does not need to be walked alone.

SHARING PROMPTS

The sharing circle is a time for the bereaved person to express their grief and be witnessed in their loss. It is a space for those holding the Circle to deeply listen and acknowledge their friend's grief, without trying to fix it or make it better.

To open the Circle, each person shares what their bereaved friend means to them and their intention for how they hope to support them through this difficult time. Share anything else that you feel called to offer into the healing Circle by means of support.

Once everyone has shared, the person whom the Circle is centred around is encouraged to take their time and speak from the heart about what they are experiencing, how the grief feels in the mind, body and soul, and anything else that they feel needs to be seen or witnessed.

Hold space for them to share all that needs to be said. In response, the group can say things like, *'I see you'*, *'I hear you'*, *'I welcome your grief'*, *'I love you'*.

PERSONAL REFLECTION

Once the sharing circle has naturally come to a close, play a beautiful song and invite people to take a pen and paper to journal privately for 5–10 minutes. Offer the writing prompt: *'If my heart could speak, it would say ...'*

RITUAL

In this ritual each person in the Circle will offer their intention to support their friend to express and share their grief. With the pouring of water, we symbolise the need for grief to flow, and give permission for emotions to be expressed and shared.

One by one, each person will come into the centre of the Circle and pour a little water from the jug into the empty bowl. As they do this, they can say, *'I pour water for your grief, may your grief keep moving and fluid. I see you.'*

Once everyone has poured water, the person who is bereaved will take the bowl of water and offer it to the earth, either outside or to a plant. With this offering, the person can ask the earth to support them and carry their tears – like a river to the sea.

CLOSE THE CIRCLE

Invite all the Women to close their eyes and to reflect upon the wisdom that the Circle has given them. For even if this Circle was in honour of [name], it was carrying important messages for everyone to receive. Take a moment for the Women to honour themselves for returning back to the Circle, to send gratitude to all the Women who gathered beside them and to honour the Woman they are gathering for.

POST-CIRCLE

Invite everyone in the Circle to set up their own little jug of water and empty bowl somewhere at home. Whenever they feel called to support their friend, they can pour a little bit of water and say aloud, *'I pour water for your grief, may your grief keep moving and fluid. I see you.'* This shared permission to let grief be deeply felt, witnessed and expressed will help emotion to remain fluid and prevent it from getting stagnant or blocked.

The individual who is grieving can also use the jug and water ritual when their own grief is feeling overwhelming. This is a beautiful way to symbolise the intention to let their emotions be felt and moved. Then once again, they can offer this water to the earth and ask for support.

BREAK-UP CIRCLE

A Circle to honour the end of a relationship

At a time when you feel your sister is struggling most, when it feels right to gather around her and offer some soul sister support

*   *   *

When a relationship ends, we aren't just saying goodbye to our partner; we are also letting go of all the dreams, plans and visions we'd created together.

The death of a relationship is so hard because the person hasn't died; they're usually just a phone call away, which can make it even more frustrating ... you're grieving the death of a relationship rather than a person. This is a time that can trigger your most painful triggers, sting your deepest wounds and call you to rise up from your very ashes.

Doing this alone is hard, and simply put, I believe we're not meant to. When we grieve a relationship there is nothing more potent than gathering with our sisters with the invitation that they witness the process alongside us.

I know so many times I've cried into a pillow with my closest girlfriends lying on my bed, cursing my former partner's very name as I eat chocolate and watch sad movies. But while that might feel good in the moment, it doesn't heal the deeper the wound.

To gather, to be witnessed, to be heard ... this is the remedy we all need.

WHO

The most supportive Women in her life

WHERE

Somewhere intimate, private, safe and sacred; ideally indoors

GATHER

- ✦ ritual basket
- ✦ 1 × fireproof bowl
- ✦ 1 × pair of scissors
- ✦ 1 × long piece of cord

Invite the griever to bring memories, photos or gifts shared with her ex.

ALTAR

Lay down your ritual cloth and place the fireproof bowl in the centre. Set out candles, crystals and anything else you feel called to. Place all other items in the ritual basket, keeping it close by.

151

OPEN THE SPACE

Introduce yourself, the practice of the Women's Circle and the intention behind why you are gathering. Smudge the Women clockwise, then yourself, and then finally the altar space. Invite each Woman to introduce themselves, and to share why they chose to be here tonight.

ENERGY TALK

During our break-up Circle, we are honouring not only the death of a relationship, but the death of all the dreams, visions and plans you made; the death of the life created together. This ending is meant to be marked, so that you can free yourself from it and slowly begin to call in what is meant for you.

By suppressing our grief, we bury it, and thus cannot move forward. This Circle will serve as a sacred space to welcome in all your feelings, emotions, fears and pain, and to bear witness to it as we support you in honouring this moment in your life, and to hold space for your grief to flow through you.

MEDITATION

Invite the Circle to close their eyes and connect with how their body feels on the seat beneath them, bringing their full presence to the holding of the ground, and acknowledging the supportive energy of Mother Earth, who is always carrying us.

Guide the grieving Woman deeper into her body by connecting her to her breath, taking three deep inhalations through the nose and out the mouth. Encourage her to welcome any feelings that are present in her body to come to the surface without judgement, inviting them into the Circle we sit in. Let her know that the Circle is holding space for her to move through any feelings, any negative thoughts, any pain, as she continues focusing on her breath.

When she's ready, invite her to bring into her mind's eye any fears, resentments or stories she's holding onto around the end of this relationship. What is she telling herself that is causing her pain and struggle? Guide her to trust whatever rises. When you sense she's ready, invite her and the Circle to return by gently feeling their bodies on the earth beneath them, and gently returning back to the space by opening their eyes.

SHARING PROMPTS

Create space for the griever to share anything that came up. What is she burying within her right now? What fears, resentments or stories are living inside of her? Give her the space to share anything coming up, reassuring her that there is no judgement and that the only way her grief can move is if she moves through it. Invite the other Women to simply witness her as she speaks, without trying to fix her. When you feel the time is right, close the sharing circle by introducing the next practice.

GRATITUDE PRACTICE

It is time to connect to gratitude. Pass the Woman a piece of paper, and ask her to tune into all that this relationship has given her. Remind her that this relationship has served her, and invite her to think back to all the good memories, all she's learnt, and all the ways she's grown through it.

She can share what's coming up, and when she's ready she will begin to write a letter of gratitude to her partner.

ORACLE CARDS

You can now shuffle the deck and ask the Woman to intuitively select a card to support her on her journey, offering any final wisdom or messages she may need. Invite her to share the card and the message within the Circle, and perhaps invite the other Women to intuit a message from the card as well.

RITUAL

Using the element of fire, we will now release all that's no longer serving her into the flame. Fire is the alchemy, it takes the dark and transmutes it into light. The ash symbolises how we rise from the fire and metamorphose.

Invite her to step up to the altar space with her letter of gratitude, her black cord, and any other memories or photographs she brought to the ceremony (only those that can be burnt).

First, the Woman can take her letter of gratitude, and with honour for all that's been, place it in the fire.

She can then take the cord and begin to burn it in the middle, as a symbol that you are energetically cutting the cord between you both. Finally, invite her to release and set fire to any of the memories, photographs or belongings that she gathered, that she is ready to let go of.

CLOSE THE CIRCLE

Invite all the Women to close their eyes and reflect upon the wisdom that the Circle has given them. For even if this Circle was in honour of [name], it was carrying important messages for everyone to receive. Take a moment for the Women to honour themselves for returning back to the Circle, to send gratitude to all the Women who gathered beside them and to send blessings to the Woman they are gathering for.

POST-CIRCLE

Welcome the Woman to take the ashes from the bowl and, in her own time, find a sacred space outdoors to scatter them onto the earth. For Mother Earth is holding you, she always is and always will be.

BABY LOSS CIRCLE

A Circle to hold space for the loss of a baby
(be it through miscarriage, abortion or stillbirth)

When the mama feels ready to be held and witnessed.
This will differ for all Women; so suggest the idea and invite her
to let you know when the time is right

*   *   *

It is estimated that between 10–25 per cent of all pregnancies result in miscarriage, and that one in three people who experience pregnancy will decide to end a pregnancy at some point in their lives.

Yet the conversation is still seen as taboo, and the number of Women who have to journey through this alone and in silence is heartbreaking. And so, I offer this space for you or for any Women in your life who have been open enough to share with you their losses.

Let us normalise what is sadly an incredibly common occurrence. Let us heal the shame that lurks around years of conditioning, so that we can truly be there for one another at the times when we need it most.

WHO

The most supportive Women in her life; those with whom she feels incredibly safe with

WHERE

Somewhere intimate, safe and sacred; indoors would typically be best. Somewhere you won't be disturbed.

GATHER

+ ritual basket
+ 1 × pack of dissolvable paper
+ 1 × bowl of water
+ 1 × tapered candle per Woman gathering

ALTAR

Lay down your ritual cloth. In the middle, place candles, crystals and anything else you feel called to. Place all other items in the ritual basket, keeping it close by.

OPEN THE SPACE

Introduce yourself, the practice of the Women's Circle and the intention behind why you are gathering. Smudge the Women clockwise, then yourself, and then finally the altar space. Invite each Woman to introduce themselves, and to share why they chose to be here tonight.

155

ENERGY TALK

A baby loss Circle is a sacred space to gather around a mama who is grieving the loss of her baby. It is a time to hold space for her, to witness her, to welcome her into a safe container through which her emotions can flow.

There is no intention for this Circle, other than to be a vessel of love for her.

MEDITATION

Invite the Circle to close their eyes, and together take three deep breaths in through the nose, and out through the mouth.

Feel yourself arriving in this sacred space, a space to honour [name] and her healing journey.

Take a moment to just become present to any feelings, sensations and emotions alive within you right now, as you just connect to holding space for them; not trying to fix or change, but simply witnessing, simply observing all that is moving within you right now.

We will bring that same presence and awareness that is within us, to the Circle. Trust that all that rises is meant to be coming through, and will reveal itself in this sacred, safe and healing container that we have all created today.

When you feel ready, gently return back to the space and open your eyes.

SHARING PROMPTS

Open the space by inviting each Woman to go around the Circle and share the strength of the grieving Woman. Express anything you feel to say that will bring her hope at this time.

Then welcome the mama to share; ask her to bring forward in this safe container anything she is feeling at this moment, any thoughts she's been thinking, any fears she's holding, any emotions that are surfacing ... anything at all. This is her space to share what she needs to share.

The best thing you can do is to lovingly witness her. Avoid trying to jump in and fix her; instead, create the safest space, allowing all that needs to come through her to come through.

ORACLE CARDS

Invite the mama to close her eyes and shuffle the deck as she calls out a prayer to the universe, as she asks for support, wisdom and a message she may need to guide her on this path.

Once she's selected her card, invite her to sit with it a moment and tune into what she feels energetically that the card is saying to her.

Invite her to share the card with the Circle, as the Circle offers any other wisdom on what they may feel the card is saying too.

RITUAL

Rituals create space to express your emotions and process your experiences in a meaningful way.

Invite the mama to write a letter to her baby, sharing anything she needs to say. Invite her to express all of her emotions, anything that came up in the Circle and anything she would like the baby to know.

She can read the letter out loud if she wishes, but if not, welcome her to just hold the letter tenderly in her arms. When she's ready, she can step over to the altar and gently release the letter into the water, watching as it dissolves and washes away.

Once she returns back to the Circle, invite each Woman to light a candle in front of them, in honour of the baby.

And once the Women in the Circle have lit their candles, welcome the mama to light hers, in honour, respect and acknowledgement of all that was, all that is and all that will be.

CLOSE THE CIRCLE

Invite all the Women to close their eyes and reflect upon the wisdom that the Circle has given them. For even if this Circle was in honour of [name], it was carrying important messages for everyone to receive. Take a moment for the Women to honour themselves for returning back to the Circle, to send gratitude to all the Women who gathered beside them and to send blessings to the Woman they are gathering for.

POST-CIRCLE

Grief is a complex journey; you're okay one minute and you're not the next. You think it's passed, only to realise it hasn't. Life is a cycle. Before you leave the space, make an oath to continue to hold space for the Woman as she journeys.

Starting a messaging group with all those present could be a supportive way to remind the Woman she is never alone. Invite her to come up with an emoji or one word that she can type to signal that she is in need of support. Set this up before you close the space.

MANIFESTATION

WISH UPON A STAR, THEY USED TO TELL ME, AND ALL YOUR DREAMS WILL COME TRUE.

As little girls we were fed the story that if you wished hard enough, all your dreams would come true, but no-one told us that the power lived in our hands. No-one taught us how to wish upon the star with intention, how to vision with meaning, how to trust that all that was meant for us would be for us, and all that wasn't would simply fall away.

There is a fine art to manifestation, to calling in all that you desire and believing it can be so. It requires a manifestation process:

☾ A dream that has come from your heartspace
☾ The ability to vision it, feel it in your bones, and experience it as if it's already happening
☾ A willingness to let go of the expectation of how and when it will appear in your life

I used to be so scared to speak about what I wanted, for fear it wouldn't happen, that I would keep my dreams locked up – so much so that I ended up hiding them away.

For words are spells, and there is a deep power that occurs when we speak what we want into being. Manifestation requires not only that you send out your wish, but also that you believe it will happen. It requires a deep trust and faith in the universe.

Sharing your dreams in the sacred container and space of the Women's Circle is the perfect way to reconnect to them, activate them and honour them. Plus, there's nothing quite like dreaming up your ideal partner with your girlfriends and then actually seeing them appear as if out of thin air ... yes, that did happen to me!

Wish upon a star my love, but just know that star is you.

THE PRAYER CIRCLE

*A Circle to call in a collective prayer for someone,
something or the world*

In the days leading up to a full moon

*   *   *

When Women gather to call in the same intention, the energy amplifies; it's like sending out a wish on steroids.

Think about it like this: when you go to a place of worship and everyone is singing the same song, the energy of the room expands, and it's thought that the message can be delivered up to the heavens more quickly.

Back in the day, Women would gather like this, to send their energy out for a specific cause to support themselves, each other or the community at large.

This Circle is about gathering for a specific reason. Perhaps someone is unwell, and you want to send out a healing prayer. Perhaps you want to support your friend in manifesting something they desire, or perhaps you feel the call to gather to send out a wish for the world.

Whatever the reason, this Circle is aimed at creating a sacred space and calling upon the power of Women gathering to manifest one specific thing.

GATHER

+ ritual basket
+ 1 × bowl of water of filtered/holy water
+ 1 × bunch of rosemary
+ 1 × cup for you

ALTAR

Lay down your ritual cloth and place your bowl of water in the centre. Create a circle of tea lights around it.

OPEN THE SPACE

Introduce yourself, the practice of the Women's Circle and the intention behind why you are gathering. Smudge the Women clockwise, then yourself, and then finally the altar space. Invite each Woman to introduce themselves and their astrology sign, and to share why they chose to be here tonight.

MEDITATION

Close your eyes, and take a moment to get settled. Take three deep breaths, in through the nose and out through the mouth, then gently welcome your natural rhythm of breathing back.

Become aware of your breath, become present to it, witnessing its ebb and flow.

Reconnect to why we've gathered in this Circle, to the single intention we all hold, the thread that holds us together in this space.

161

Call it in, feel it, vision it, believe it to be so, for when we work together with our collective energy we can make mountains move.

Commit to staying present throughout the Circle, so that we can use the power of our energy together to bring this wish into being. When you feel ready, very gently open your eyes and step back into the Circle.

SHARING PROMPTS

Open the sharing circle by sharing a few of these prompts, and inviting the Women to connect on the deepest level regarding why they are here. Create space to journal what's coming up for them, or simply to share in the Circle.

+ Why have we gathered tonight?
+ What is the intention for the Circle?
+ What is the vision or dream we are wishing to cultivate?

If it is a manifestation of one Woman in the Circle, invite her to speak what she is seeking to call in. If it is a collective intention for the world, or a crisis, then allow each Woman the space to share what they want to send out in the Circle.

Once the sharing has taken place, simplify the intention to one sentence. For example, *'I am calling in healing for* [insert name].' *'We are manifesting an immediate resolution for ...'* You want to be specific, but simple, so the message will be carried in a clear way.

In order to manifest this, each Woman must truly feel the energy in her whole being. This is a prayer, a thought that we are alchemising to become a thing. It is a practice of putting aside our own ego for the good of all as we step into our true essence of oneness.

ORACLE CARDS

Invite each Woman to pull a card with the intention of receiving deeper information about what energy is needed to support this wish in manifesting.

+ What can I do to support the manifestation of this wish?
+ What do we need to let go of in order to make it so?

Share the cards with the Circle and any messages that came through.

RITUAL

Reconnecting back to the intention, invite each Woman one by one to step up to the bowl of water. Speak the intention into the bowl as you drop a sprig of rosemary into the water. Rosemary holds the energy of memory, and can carry our wishes along for us.

When everyone returns back to the Circle, hold hands, close your eyes, and each hold the vision in your mind's eye.

One by one, speak the simplified vision out loud, sending it out into the bowl of water and up to the universe.

Once everyone has spoken, together repeat the manifestation three times, and then pass around the bowl of water, inviting each Woman to take a sip from the bowl as you seal its energy into the cells of your being with belief, with a knowing that it will be so.

Take a deep breath in, and exhale out.
Take a deep breath in, and exhale out.
Take a deep breathe in, and exhale out.

And so it is.

CLOSE THE CIRCLE

Invite the Women to close their eyes, to reconnect back to the wisdom that the Circle has given them. Take a moment for the Women to honour themselves for committing to this collective intention, to send gratitude to all the Women who gathered beside them in the Circle and to the energy of the universe for making it so.

RITES OF PASSAGE

MAIDEN • MAMA • CRONE

RITES OF PASSAGE are a series of initiations we as Women are called to journey through on our path, with every step leading us deeper and deeper into ourselves, our power and our connection to the feminine. Rites of passage were found and honoured in almost every ancient culture, yet have been lost and forgotten in Western culture. So this is a calling to welcome our daughters, our sisters, our mothers and our grandmothers back to the village. Are you ready to step back in?

MAIDEN

ALL THE FLOWERS OF ALL THE TOMORROWS,
ARE IN THE SEEDS OF TODAY.

Likened to the energy of spring or a crescent moon, the maiden represents curiosity, vitality, excitement, innocence, excitement and magik.
A time of lightness, a time of becoming, a time of play.

The road that lies ahead of the maiden is full of potential. Nothing is certain, everything is possible.

What a beautiful time to offer the maidens in your life wisdom and guidance.

We will begin to highlight how we as mamas, or guardians for the next generation of Women, can introduce the magik of the Circle to them early.

I can think of truly nothing more important than passing down the tools to the Women to come, for this is how it always would have been.

So here are a few ways you can get started, and weave the magik of the Circle into the lives of the little Maiden's in your life.

LITTLE MAIDEN'S CIRCLE

Intentional birthday parties

On her birthday

*　　　*　　　*

Birthday parties are the perfect celebration to welcome the art of the Circle into your little girl's life. We all understand the importance of celebrating a birthday; however, could we make this day that little bit more magikal? More symbolic? More meaningful?

A big part of what is so lacking in our culture is the lost art of community. These days, children miss out on being witnessed intimately by others. This Circle creates a space for close-knit family and friends to acknowledge the growth, change and transformation of a child each year.

They've been witnessed ... they are being shown their uniqueness, their gifts, their light, and this is the value of being brought up in a village.

Little Women's Circles create a magical space to celebrate, acknowledge and honour the child's spin around the sun each year. So here are some ideas on how you can create your own for your little one.

WHO

Her closest female family members and friends

WHERE

At the birthday girl's house, or somewhere familiar to her

GATHER

Birthday parties are typically themed, decorating the space in alignment to what the child is drawn to. My invitation for you would be to find the deeper meaning behind what she's drawn to, and to weave it in more symbolically.

Let her participate in the gathering and creation of the space if she chooses, explaining what each symbol represents.

For example, if she loves fairies, perhaps you create a fairy Circle and share with her some beautiful stories about fairies and the energy they hold. Or if she is drawn to sport, perhaps you can share with her the drive and power of working together.

Ask her what activity she'd like to do during her party, or if she's too young, choose something you know she'd enjoy, such as painting, sports, drawing, collage, artwork, knitting, jewellery, clay.

Gather all the equipment you will need for this.

Remember, everything has a hidden meaning behind it, so let your child guide you and then create the sacredness through that.

Invite the Women to bring an intentional birthday gift.

ALTAR

Lay down your ritual cloth and create a flower circle in the middle (invite your daughter to help you prepare it). Weave in any symbols and decoration that she connects to. Fill your ritual basket with her crafts of choice and keep it close.

OPEN THE SPACE

Introduce yourself, the practice of the Women's Circle and the intention behind why you are gathering. Make the space feel sacred, but also age-appropriate; smudge if you feel called to do so. Invite each Woman to introduce themselves and to explain how they know the birthday girl.

ENERGY TALK

This could be a nice time for the mama to talk about the birthday girl, perhaps sharing why she chose to hold this Circle and how meaningful and special this space can be.

MEDITATION

Invite the Circle to keep their eyes open or, if they feel called to, to close their eyes, holding hands in a circle as they bring the child into their mind's eye.

Tune into the energy of this child, tune into all that they've brought to your life this year, to all that they've stepped into and achieved physically, emotionally, mentally and spiritually. Bring forward any memories you've shared with the child into your mind's eye. Allow yourself to receive the gifts, lessons and teachings this child has offered you this year; trust whatever comes through. Before opening your eyes, take a few moments to send deep heart gratitude to this child, and to call in any blessing you may have for her as she prepares for this next spin around the sun.

SHARING PROMPTS

Go around the Circle one by one, sharing:

+ One thing they have noticed change about the child this year
+ One thing they love about the child
+ One thing they're grateful for about the child
+ One memory they have of the child this year

BIRTHDAY PRACTICE

Together, create something for the child, such as a drawing, collage, artwork, knitting, jewellery or clay. Use this practice as a way to express the child's energy this year, and to seal any blessings and wishes for the child, using your hands, and intention.

Place your creation in a birthday basket as a symbol of the age of the child. Each year, you can revisit what you created the year before, and see how the child has changed, evolved and grown.

RITUAL

Invite the Circle to connect to a blessing for the child for this year.

One by one, each person in the Circle can step over to the birthday girl, sharing their gift with her and any blessing/wishes they have for her year ahead.

Once all the gifts have been given, invite the birthday girl to take a few moments to think of what she's grateful for, and any wishes she has for the year ahead.

Then bring her birthday cake out, and before blowing out her candles, invite her to speak her wishes and gratitude list out to the Circle. Remember, contrary to what the folktales may say, your dreams cannot be taken away when spoken; rather, they fly when shared in a sacred circle.

CLOSE THE CIRCLE

End the Circle with a tea party to feast on the joyous celebration that is another spin around the sun.

1ST MOON CIRCLE

A ceremony to mark her Womanhood

Start of young girl's first bleed

*　　　*　　　*

Across all ancient cultures, when a young girl becomes a Woman, it marked the first rite of passage in the journey of the feminine. For as she enters Womanhood, so do the seeds of life present themselves.

Sadly, in our culture we have not only lost the art of celebrating this initiation, but we have become conditioned to feel shame and hide it away. We must instil in our daughters the sacredness of their moon-time, so they can be empowered to connect with it. For it is within these times that we find our true power.

So this is a calling to reclaim our feminine cycles, by holding a 1st moon circle.

Learning to celebrate and welcome their cycles, along with teaching girls how to navigate and equip them with tools to support their unfolding, is so important.

To create sacred spaces for them go inwards, to empower them to use their moontime as a time to retreat, to step away from the outside world, to pause, to come home, to be still.

This circle is an invitation to introduce beautiful nourishing ways to honour her bleed, in order to prepare them for a lifetime of honouring the ebbs and flows of the feminine.

For I truly believe if you treat her like a goddess, she will feel like one.

WHO

Her closest female family members and friends

GATHER

+ 1 × bunch of red roses
+ 1 × moontime basket*
+ 1 × moonstone
+ 1 × herbal blend (salts, petals, herbs)
+ 1 × cauldron or glass bowl
+ 1 × red cloth

*A moontime basket is a collection of nourishing and healing things that each month you gather to use during your bleed. For example, in my moontime basket, I collect things throughout the month, such as my favourite chocolate bar, a pair of comfy knickers and a hot water bottle. I may write a little note to myself during the month, or put my favourite poetry book in there.

Then, when I come onto my bleed, I collect my moontime basket and it serves as a gift that I can bring myself, filled with nourishing treats that I have gathered to honour this sacred time for myself.

Invite the Women to bring something to contribute to the moontime basket, such as:

+ a soft blanket or cloth
+ crystal
+ hot water bottle
+ chocolate
+ something lovely to do during moontime bleeds, such as a colouring book
+ candle
+ underwear, cosy PJs
+ poem or letter

ALTAR

Creating a womb-like moon cave would serve this gathering well. Lay your ritual cloth down, then create a flower circle using red roses, and fill the spaces with tea lights. Place the red cloth at the seat of the young girl and ensure the room is dimly lit. Light some beautiful incense.

OPEN THE SPACE

Introduce yourself, the practice of the Women's Circle and the intention behind why you are gathering. Make the space feel sacred, but also age-appropriate; smudge if you feel called to do so. Invite each Woman to introduce themselves and to explain how they know the young Woman.

ENERGY TALK

Introduce the concept of moontime. Moontime is a more sacred way to talk about your menstruation and time of bleed. It is a gift from nature; a moment every month when we are given permission to step away from our everyday lives, to nourish, treat and cleanse ourselves. It is a time to slow down and retreat. It is a time that can hold great power for Women, a time when we are most connected to the natural world.

When we honour this time as Women, we create the space to renew ourselves and come back into the world filled with vitality and energy. This time is so important. Welcome to your moontime. This is the beginning of your journey into the magikal realm of Womanhood.

Share the moontime basket with the young Woman, the gifts the Circle has given her and the practice of gathering her own sacred tools each month to support her in her moontime.

MEDITATION

Take three deep breaths, inhaling through the nose and through the mouth. Welcoming all the Women to ground into this space, to arrive, to connect to the intentions behind why they are here; to honour [name]'s first moontime.

Taking three deep breaths, inhaling through the nose and out the mouth, set the intention to come back into the space with presence, to all that is.

SHARING PROMPTS

Create the space for the young girl to share any fears, concerns or apprehension she has around her bleed. Welcome any practical or emotional questions she may have.

Then invite the Circle to open as each Woman shares what they love about being a Woman, empowering the young girl to welcome this rite of passage into her life with positivity and grace.

ORACLE CARDS

Invite each Woman to pull a card for the young girl, setting the intention to receive a powerful message to support her on her journey to becoming a Woman. Once each Woman has selected a card, invite the Women to go around sharing the message they received for her.

RITUAL

One by one, invite each Woman to go into the centre of the Circle, gathering a small handful of salts and herbs. Invite her to sprinkle it into the bowl as she whispers a wish for the young girl into the blend.

Welcome the young girl to watch as these powerful Women in her life cast this potion for her.

Once each Woman has infused their wish into the salts, return back to the Circle and sprinkle rose flowers over her, as you celebrate, adorn and welcome her into Womanhood.

Perhaps bring her some yummy, nourishing food to eat, then sit in the Circle eating, feasting and celebrating.

CLOSE THE CIRCLE

Invite the Women to close their eyes, to reconnect back to the wisdom that the Circle has given them. Take a moment to honour [name] and the start of her Womanhood journey, to thank all the Women who gathered for creating the sacred space, and to Mama Moon for blessing this child on her journey.

POST-CIRCLE

Once everyone leaves, Mama or guardian creates a sacred ritual bath for the young Woman; lighting the candles in the bathroom, preparing a sacred space for her daughter, drawing the bath and infusing it with the salts created at the Circle.

COMING-OF-AGE CIRCLE

*A Circle to celebrate and support a
Woman's coming of age*

Upon turning 16, 18, 21, or whenever you would typically
celebrate a coming of age in your culture

*   *   *

In Western culture, coming of age is typically defined by when you're legally allowed to drink, as if that is the defining factor of becoming an adult. I look back to my coming of age, my eighteenth birthday party, when I felt grown up enough to go to a nightclub with some girlfriends, only to come home and spend the rest of night with my head in a toilet. Oh, sweet maiden. Of course, these experiences teach us, shape us – and make us laugh ten years later, on reflection.

But something inside me questions our culture's initiation into adulthood. My feeling is, we can do better than this.

The coming-of-age Circle is a welcoming into the blossoming period of a young Woman, with the intention to not only celebrate, honour and acknowledge her, but also to equip her with all the tools she may need on her journey.

As a young Woman, having a space to be witnessed, understood and heard is huge. I know how much I longed for it. I believe that if we consciously create these spaces for Women at the start of their journeys, they will bring these practices into all parts of their lives moving forward. The work has to start here. This is how we raise a generation of embodied, empowered and magikal Women.

WHO

Your closest female family members and friends

GATHER

+ your ritual basket
+ 1 × chalice
+ anything you want to give her for her ritual basket
+ 1 × wine cup per Woman
+ 1 × bottle of champagne/wine/non-alcoholic drink
+ 1 × bunch of seasonal flowers

Invite all the Women to add an item to her ritual basket. Examples include:

+ smudge tool
+ sacred feather
+ shell
+ symbolic charm or piece of jewellery
+ oracle or tarot deck
+ journal

OPEN THE SPACE

Introduce yourself, the practice of the Women's Circle and the intention behind why you are gathering. Smudge the Women clockwise, then yourself, and then finally the altar space. Invite each Woman to introduce themselves and their astrology sign, and to share how they know the young Woman, and why it's important that they gather.

ENERGY TALK

As you enter Womanhood, you will begin the deeper journey that the feminine calls you to. In your maiden years you are given the space to explore, to be curious, to play, to find yourself ... we are here for you on the journey, and will be walking beside you as you navigate your maid years. In this space we will introduce you to the true art of the Women's Circle, a safe, sacred space for you to return to whenever you need it.

Gift her the ritual basket, and perhaps each Woman can go around sharing what they bought her and why ...

MEDITATION

Invite the maiden to begin to tune into anything that's on her mind, connecting to her breath and welcoming her to sit with anything causing discomfort, worry or anxiety, no matter how big or small.

Invite the other Women in the Circle to begin to tune into their breath, and to begin reflect on their own Womanhood journey. What are some of the lessons they've learnt? What tools have been supportive and served you?

Bring them out of the meditation when you feel ready, and invite them to write down anything that came up.

SHARING PROMPTS

Invite the maiden to share any fears she has around the Circle. Allow her to speak them into the ether without needing to be fixed by anyone.

Create a safe container for her by welcoming everyone to witness her with love.

Once she's shared, perhaps invite each Woman to go around the Circle and share a bit about their own journey of Womanhood, how they deal with worries, anxiety, etc. They might share:

+ One piece of advice you have for her on her journey ahead
+ One lesson you've learnt on your path
+ One tool to pass on to help her navigate life

This Circle is about empowering the young Woman to know that all she needs lies within her, so share some wisdom and tools with her to support her in accessing her own power.

ORACLE CARDS

Invite the young Woman to pull a card from her new deck. Show her how to read it, invite her to find her own meaning and message from this card, and then go around the Circle inviting each Woman to interpret what they feel her card means, or invite them to pull a card for her as well and read it to her.

RITUAL

Connect to a blessing you have for the maiden; wisdom, or a message you want her to pass on during her journey.

Pour a glass of wine/champagne/non-alcoholic drink into your own cups and into the chalice. Pass the chalice around the Circle, and as you each hold it, whisper blessings, wishes and messages into it.

Once it's gone around the whole Circle, present it to the maiden. Invite her to whisper a blessing she has for herself into it, before all raising your glasses and clinking them together, as you toast and drink in the journey of her Womanhood; may it all be sealed with intentions.

POST-CIRCLE

Have a feast to celebrate this Woman and the gifts she's been given in the Circle, and the basket full of tools to support her on her journey.

MAMA

AT SOME POINT IN HER LIFE, EACH WOMAN WILL BE ASKED TO CROSS THE THRESHOLD FROM MAIDEN TO MOTHER.

When I use these words, I speak of the actual and archetypal mother. For the energy of the Mother is one who is called to devote herself to something higher than herself. She is the vessel, the carrier, the caretaker of life itself.

It is here, on the cusp of transforming from Maiden to Mother, that one of the deepest initiations of the feminine arises: the quest to journey to the depths of oneself, to meet parts of you that you didn't even know existed, in order to be reborn anew.

As such, here we pay homage to the ancient traditions and rituals that knew how important it was to honour, celebrate and witness a Woman on the brink of Mamahood.

They say it takes a village to make a Mama, so let's remember how we can create that village for the Women in our lives.

BRIDAL BLESSING

An alternative bachelorette party

In the lead-up to the wedding day

*　　　　*　　　　*

I include bridal blessings in the Mamahood journey, for I believe the energy of the Mama is the one who devotes her life to something or someone else. We can see this journey beginning to emerge when we make the conscious commitment to marry someone.

The ritual of marriage is one that has withstood the test of time. It is a universal celebration that we honour, witness and acknowledge across all cultures. However, typically in the Western world, we have been swept up with the frills of it, forgetting the sacred initiation that is calling us.

I remember as I was planning my wedding, how easy it was to direct my anxiety towards the table plans and wedding dresses. But as I looked closer, I realised I was using all of this as a way to distract myself from sitting with the energy that was churning inside of me, calling me to acknowledge the deep transformation that was occurring as I prepared to devote myself to my partner.

I realised I needed more support, so I gathered my sisters, asking if they would form a bride tribe around me. I didn't long for bridesmaids to come dress shopping with, I deeply longed for my sisters to gather around me.

And so, instead of a bachelorette party, I had a bridal blessing. The night before my wedding we gathered in Circle and they held space for me, to connect back to myself, to sit with my fears, to honour the journey I was about to embark on and to celebrate my next step.

Nothing has ever felt more fulfilling, and so I share with you the alternative bachelorette party. A sacred space for your bride tribe to gather, honour and celebrate you before you take that sacred walk down the aisle.

WHO

The bride tribe and important Women in the bride's life

GATHER

+ ritual basket
+ 3 × pillar candles
+ white flowers to make a flower circle (such as baby's breath, hydrangeas, daisies)
+ 1 × craft tag per Woman
+ 1 × long ribbon
+ 1 × fireproof bowl

Invite each Woman to bring a flower that reminds her of the bride-to-be.

ALTAR

Place down your ritual cloth and position your three pillar candles in a circle in the centre. Create a beautiful white flower circle around them. Keep the fireproof bowl and your ritual basket close by.

OPEN THE SPACE

Introduce yourself, the practice of the Women's Circle and the intention behind why you are gathering. Smudge the Women clockwise, then yourself, and then finally the altar space. Invite each Woman to introduce themselves and their astrology sign, and to share how they know the bride-to-be.

ENERGY TALK

A bridal blessing is a sacred space created to honour, support and celebrate the bride-to-be as she transitions into marriage. We gather around her to hold space for her as she prepares for the next step of her journey; and to remind her that she is never alone.

MEDITATION

Invite the Women to close their eyes, connect to their breath, and to bring their full presence, energy and attention to this space. The greatest gift you can bring to the bride in this Circle is your full attention.

Use this as a time to ground, and come back into yourself, letting go of anything from your day you may be carrying.

Begin to visualise the bride in your mind's eye.

Welcome her into your awareness, as you bring forward the first time you met her.

Welcome that vision in, and then begin call in times when she's supported you, times when she's made you laugh, when she was there for you, held you, inspired you, celebrated you.

Let these memories fill your being with the love you hold for her, as we set the intention to hold space for her today as she embarks on the next chapter of her life.

SHARING PROMPTS

The sharing circle is a time to shine the bride's light back to her. So rarely in our culture do we get the opportunity to truly hear how we have shaped and changed someone's life. This is a time where you, as the bride tribe, can truly shine light onto the bride and show her how special she is in your life.

This can be emotional (make sure the tissues are close). One by one, introduce yourself in the Circle. Share the flower you have chosen and why it reminds you of the bride. Share any memories with the bride that came through in the meditation. Share anything else that you love about the bride.

Once everyone has gone around the Circle, invite the bride to connect to anything she wants to share, any fears she has around the wedding or marriage, and anything that she feels called to let go of before she walks down the aisle. Hold space for her as she shares anything that comes up.

Invite her to write down what she's ready to let go of, and to burn it in the candle at the centre of the altar.

This is a sacred moment for her to let go of anything she feels is no longer serving her, and it's a sacred moment for you to witness her doing this.

ORACLE CARDS

Now it's time to bless the bride.

Using the cards, we will set the intention to receive a blessing for the bride; some guidance, inspiration or any messages she may need to support her on the journey that lies ahead.

Once everyone has pulled a card, spend some time tuning into what the message might be, and then share your cards and the message you received in the Circle with the bride.

RITUAL

In this ritual we will be creating a bridal bouquet for the bride, using the flowers each Woman brought.

Give each Woman a craft tag for her to write down a blessing she has for the bride and the journey that awaits her; perhaps inspired by the Oracle card they received.

Then one by one, gather the flower you brought from the altar space, tie your blessing to the stem, and step over to the bride, sealing your blessing into the flower as you offer your flower blessing to her.

Once everyone has circled around the bride, giving her their flowers, you can invite the bride to hold up her bouquet, to tie a ribbon around it tightly and to rise up as she extends her bouquet up to the sky.

POST-CIRCLE

Invite the bride-to-be to dry her bouquet in a dark cupboard, and to weave some of the flowers or the ribbon from the bouquet into her bridal bouquet. This will serve as a support and magik for her as she walks down the aisle, reminding her that her sisters have her back.

You can close with a beautiful feast, to celebrate the bride.

MAMA BLESSING

An alternative baby shower

During the Mama's third trimester

*　　　*　　　*

For me, a Mama Circle is the most profound space I have ever sat in. To witness, hold space, and celebrate a Woman on the cusp of motherhood is so sacred and so important.

In this Circle, we can truly support a mama-to-be in remembering her strength, power, divinity and anything else she may need as she prepares to birth not only her baby, but herself as a Mother.

In ancient communities, these spaces were common. The Native American tribes call them Blessingways, and we see threads of them in the form of baby showers in our more Western approach to celebrating motherhood.

This Circle, much like the bridal blessings, will pay respect to the ancient ways, as we revive the art of gathering in a Circle to honour, support, and celebrate the Mama as she sits between the worlds, preparing to transition.

It is the intention of this Circle to offer the Mama the space to remember her power, to let go of any fears, to be seen, witnessed, celebrated and honoured for the journey she is embarking on, one that will change her forever. They say it takes a village to make a Mama; this Circle is here to remind her that although only she can birth her baby, she is not alone on the quest.

WHO

Her closest female friends and family

GATHER

+ ritual basket
+ 3 × bunches of flowers in full bloom (such as roses, sunflowers, dahlias)
+ 1 × tea light for each Woman
+ 1 × bundle of hemp cord
+ 1 × pair of scissors

Invite each Woman to bring a meaningful and symbolic bead of their choice.

ALTAR

Lay down your ritual cloth. Create a beautiful full and abundant flower circle in the centre, and dot the tea lights around it. Keep the cord and scissors close by in your ritual basket.

OPEN THE SPACE

Introduce yourself, the practice of the Women's Circle and the intention behind why you are gathering. Smudge the Women clockwise, then yourself, and then finally the altar space. Invite each Woman to introduce themselves and their astrology sign, and to share how they know the mama-to-be.

ENERGY TALK

A Mama blessing is a gathering to celebrate, honour and support the mama-to-be as she prepares for her most profound journey yet. As we gather around her, we create a sacred space for her to be witnessed, acknowledged, seen and heard, supporting her in remembering her power, strength and divinity. Remember, it takes a village to make a Mama; you are not alone.

MEDITATION

Invite the Women to close their eyes, connect to their breath, and to bring their full presence, energy and attention to this space. The greatest gift you can bring to the mama-to-be in this Circle is your full attention.

Use this as a time to ground, and come back into yourself, letting go of anything from your day that you may be carrying.

Begin to visualise the mama-to-be in your mind's eye.

Welcome her into your awareness, as you bring forward the first time you met her. Welcome that vision in, and then begin call in times when she's supported you, times when she's made you laugh, when she was there for you, held you, inspired you, celebrated you.

Let these memories fill your being with the love you hold for her. Tune into the light she carries and all that she has passed on to you, as we set the intention to remind her of the power she holds within, of all the strength she keeps, and the gifts that live within her.

SHARING PROMPTS

This sharing circle is a time to celebrate the mama-to-be.

One by one, go around the Circle sharing with her all the light that you see in her, reminding her of her power, gifts and strength.

Once everyone has shared, and the Mama is filled up with light, you can now invite her to tune into any fears, anxieties or worries she is holding around her pregnancy, birth or journey into motherhood.

Allow space and time for her to write any fears down and, if she feels called, invite her to share with the Circle. Then once she feels whole, ask her to step to the altar and burn the paper she wrote her fears down on, as she exhales deeply out through her mouth.

ORACLE CARDS

Pass the deck of cards around, and invite each Woman to select one, with the intention of receiving a blessing for the Mama on her journey. Trust that you will receive the energy she needs to support her.

RITUAL

Invite each Woman to connect to the blessings they hold for the mama-to-be, tuning into any wisdom you seek to pass on to her, any advice or support you may have for her, any intention you wish to give to her.

Gather the hemp cord from the altar space and begin to pass the cord around the Circle. Invite each Woman to gather their beads, to share why they brought the bead and the blessing they have for her as they thread their beads onto the string, passing the cord around until each Woman has threaded her blessing bead.

Once it reaches the Mama, cut and tie the cord three times to seal the power and energy into the string. The blessing beads are now sealed with wishes, blessings and the energy of the Circle, and can be worn or held or throughout the rest of the pregnancy and in the birthing room, too.

Before closing the Circle, invite each Woman to gather a tea light from the centre of the altar. You will be invited to light this candle when the Mama goes into labour.

POST-CIRCLE

Here are some other powerful ways you can help the Mama feel supported throughout the rest of her pregnancy, birth and postpartum:

+ Set up a birthing messaging group with all the Women present at the Circle. Select one Woman closest to the Mama, who can let the others know when the Mama has gone into labour. It is then you will be asked to light your candles, and make a wish for the Mama as she steps through this powerful initiation.
+ Instead of baby gifts, perhaps invite each Woman to cook a meal for the Mama once the baby has been born. You can set up a meal train post-Circle, finding out the type of food she would love, and commit to a day or days you can bring this to her.

BABY BLESSING

An alternative naming ceremony

After the first forty days postpartum

*　　　　*　　　　*

I like to think of this one as an alternative to a christening or more traditional naming ceremony.

When I was pregnant with my daughter, Luna, I knew I wanted to create a sacred space for her to be welcomed into the world. I honoured the first forty days, which is a tradition maintained across many cultures that asks the Woman to stay at home, to go very gently and slowly, in order to heal, to bond and to truly begin to embody this huge transformation that has occurred.

It is said that in the first forty days postpartum, you and your child are still very much in between the worlds. This is a sacred time for the two of you to bond, connect and receive each other. The forty days gives you the space to go slowly, gently and move in your own time, being held by the comfort of your own home.

It creates space, so that when you are ready, you both can step out into the world together, reborn, as mother and child.

This Circle creates an opportunity to honour that welcoming. To gather the Women who have supported you on your journey into motherhood, to tell them the tales of your birth, to share with them the ups and downs of the path so far and to bless you and your baby.

WHO

The Women who have supported her on her motherhood journey, including, of course, mother and child

GATHER

+ ritual basket
+ flowers that represent babies, children and mothers (such as fresh daffodils, baby's breath, daisies)
+ 1 × flower crown for Mama
+ a collection of beads, symbols and talismans to add to the dream catcher
+ 1 × wooden craft hoop

Invite each Woman to bring a symbol that they can weave onto the dream catcher or baby mobile, such as a feather, charm, bead or crystal.

ALTAR

Lay down your ritual cloth. Create a flower circle in the centre, and weave any symbols and objects for the dream catcher into the circle. Place the flower crowns for Mama and baby on their cushions.

OPEN THE SPACE

Introduce yourself, the practice of the Women's Circle and the intention behind why you are gathering. Smudge the Women clockwise, then yourself, and then finally the altar space. Avoid using sage, as the smell and smoke will be too harsh for a baby. Instead, consider using Palo Santo; you won't need to smudge the baby. Invite each Woman to introduce themselves and their astrology sign, to share why they chose to be here and to place their symbols on the altar.

ENERGY TALK

The baby blessing is a sacred space created to welcome both Mama and baby back into the world. It's a space for the Mama to share her journey so far, to be seen, witnessed, welcomed and celebrated ... and for the baby to be showered with love, high vibrational energy and blessings to send them out into the world together.

MEDITATION

Conduct a short meditation to ground everybody into the space. Invite them to connect with their breath, to visualise the air going in through the nose and out through the mouth. Welcome each Woman to settle into the space as they prepare intentionally to welcome Mama and baby back from their birthing journey and into the world.

SHARING PROMPTS

Create the space for Mama to present her child to the Circle; invite the Mama to share the baby's name, and any symbolism woven into it.

Then create the space for Mama to share her birth story. Creating a space to recount it, and to have it heard and witnessed by others is so immensely powerful.

Invite the Mama to open the sharing by sharing the story of her birth, from start to finish. Encourage her to share as much detail as she feels comfortable with, and create a safe container by listening with love and focus.

Once she's shared her birth story, create the space for her to share anything that has been coming up on her Mamahood journey so far, anything she's been struggling with, anything she needs support with, anything at all.

Open out the space for everyone else to offer some words of wisdom, support or encouragement for the Mama.

PRACTICE

This may be a nice time to adorn Mama. Someone else can hold the baby while Mama receives a foot rub, a massage, and her flower crown.

ORACLE CARDS

Pass the deck of cards around, and invite each Woman to select one, with the intention of receiving a blessing for Mama and baby. Trust that you will receive the energy she needs to support her.

RITUAL

Create your dream catcher or baby mobile.

Tune into the blessing you hold for Mama and baby. One by one, rise as you pass around the frame for the dream catcher or the baby mobile, and weave your charm or symbol into the frame, sealing your wish and blessing for Mama and baby into it.

Step over to baby and Mama give them a hug or kiss as you vocally share your blessing with them.

Once each Woman has woven their blessing in, present the baby gift to Mama and baby.

POST CIRCLE

Welcome the Mama to hang the dream catcher over the bed where the baby sleeps, as a symbol of protection and blessings. Reminding both Mama and Baby how loved, held and supported they are.

CRONE

THE CRONE IS THE FINAL THRESHOLD
A WOMAN IS CALLED TO STEP OVER
IN HER JOURNEY OF THE FEMININE.

It is symbolised by the end of her bleed. This phase is typically marked by a few events: menopause, eldership and finally death. These are the rites of passage calling us, beckoning us and asking us to step through them in order to truly embody our life's purpose and lessons.

There is a difference between getting older and becoming an elder. Stepping into the energy of the crone enables us to, with grace, take time to reflect, harvest and review our life's work, to tend to any last healing that is coming through, so at the end of our lives we can rest knowing that we have done what we came here to do.

Sadly, in our culture, the reverence for the crone period has been forgotten. Instead, we seek to stay eternally young, and in doing so we hide the wrinkles on our faces, the ones that are trying to lead us back to our power.

We have forgotten that the old are our elders; that they are the wisdom we seek. We've stopped listening to their stories, receiving their light, and in doing so we have lost generational healing.

Even they have forgotten their place, for we hide the hags away, but in doing so we block the most sacred power of the feminine.

This chapter is about reclaiming the crone; celebrating, honouring, revering, holding space and listening to the elders in our lives.

For it is in their final years, and in the legacy they leave, that the feminine heals.

MENOPAUSAL CIRCLE

*A circle to honour a Woman who is stepping
through the passage of menopause*

Two years after she's stopped bleeding

*   *   *

196

This circle was passed down and adapted by wise Woman Jane Hardwicke Collings, and the energy of the crone was transmitted by my dear mentor Fiona Arrigo. Thank you, wise Women.

This sacred gathering honours the ending of our bleeding years. This is a rite of passage in the journey of the feminine that acknowledges the energy, the power and the life we have given from our first moon to our last moon. We gather together to celebrate, honour and support the Women in our lives who our stepping across this most powerful threshold.

Our modern culture, dominated by its quick-fix mentality and disconnection from nature, has labelled peri-menopause and menopause as a series of unwanted and even dangerous symptoms that are to be avoided. Medication has been created to bypass the process, encouraging Women to avoid the physical, emotional and psychological aspects of this significant rite of passage. We have been conditioned to be ashamed of this time, and its true medicine has been hidden from us. It's almost as if our culture has wanted us to stay eternally young, keeping us from the power we step into as we ripen.

For it is said that when a Woman stops menstruating, she holds her wise blood, therefore increasing her wisdom. This time can be seen as another labour in a Woman's life – however, this time she gives birth to herself, a new version of herself.

For too long, menstruation, childbirth and menopause, the three main rites of passage for a Woman, have ceased to be respected, contributing to the wounded feminine in our modern world. Through celebrating, honouring and knowing the wisdom of the cycles, we can help heal the wounded feminine in ourselves and in our world.

Honouring menopause and reclaiming this rite of passage is fundamental for the healing of the feminine, and the reclamation of the true power of the wise Woman within.

WHO

Her closest female family members and friends

GATHER
+ ritual basket
+ 1 × fire pit
+ a bunch of dark red flowers

- 1 × dried flower wreath for each honoured Woman
- 1 × special cushion to be placed beside the altar for each

Woman being honoured to be seated on during the ceremony

Invite the Women to bring something meaningful to add to the altar; something from nature.

ALTAR

Lay your ritual cloth down, place the small fire pit on top of it in the centre of the space and light the fire, then place all the red flower stems around the fire pit. Place the flower wreath on her special cushion; ready to await her. Place the ritual basket beside the altar, and place any offerings from nature with the circle.

OPEN THE SPACE

Introduce yourself, the practice of the Women's Circle and the intention behind why you are gathering. Smudge the Women clockwise, then yourself, and then finally the altar space. Invite each Woman to introduce themselves and their astrology sign, and to share how they know the Woman we are honouring.

ENERGY TALK

This is a gathering to honour (name/s) and to welcome her to the next season of Womanhood, her Autumn season, Maga, Menopause.

Moving from the Mother season to the Maga season is a huge shift, a metaphoric labour known as the 'change of life'.

This time, this labour, is a time of vast self-learning, resulting in a birth, as labours do. This time the birth is of a new Woman, changed.

Autumn, as we know from the trees, is the time for letting go of things that are no longer useful, and the time of the harvest. The fruits that were growing in the summer are now ready.

As your friends, your companions on the journey of Womanhood, we acknowledge you for your rebirth into this fruitful season of your life.

MEDITATION

Invite the Circle to close their eyes, and gently begin to ground into the space, taking three deep inhalations, in through the nose and out through the mouth. Feel your bodies getting heavier and heavier as you ground into the earth beneath you. Beginning to tune in to the Woman we have gathered to honour today, bring her into your mind's eye, as we prepare to honour, celebrate and support her on this new step of her journey.

What have you learnt from this Woman? Can you reflect on all that she has brought to you, and to the world since you've known her? (Pause for at least three minutes to allow for any visions and memories to come through.)

How are you watching her change and alchemise? What do you see in her that you feel she is now ready to offer the world? (Pause for at least three minutes to allow for any visions and memories to come through.)

What one wish or blessing do you hold for her? (Pause for at least one minute to allow for any visions and memories to come through.)

When you feel you have gathered all that you wish to share with her, feel yourself coming back to your seat, back to this physical sacred space, and when you feel ready, very gently open your eyes.

SHARING PROMPTS

Open the sharing circle by inviting each Woman to share what came through in the meditation. Invite the Woman you are honouring to listen and receive with an open heart, taking in all the medicine she has given to the world through the words of the Women around her.

ORACLE CARDS

Invite the Woman you are honouring to receive the deck of cards and to shuffle them, asking to receive a message from the universe, to call forward an energy she is being asked to step into as she journeys towards the wise Woman within. Encourage her to intuitively pull the card that calls to her, and then read the card to the Circle and invite anyone else to offer an interpretation as to what it might be reflecting back.

RITUAL

This ritual is about honouring and giving gratitude to the sacredness of her blood, the blood that created life, that gave so many blessings to the world. As she lets go of all that has been, she can welcome all that is waiting for her.

Invite the Woman to step towards the firepit wearing her flower crown, and to collect the flowers that lay around it. Invite her to take the petals from the flowers one by one and release them into the flames, whispering (or speaking aloud) all that she is grateful for, all that she's ready to let go of and all that she's ready to call in as she welcomes this new season of her life.

Let her words and intentions seal into the fire; and let the fire remind her that she holds the same power within her to alchemise and transform all that she wishes to.

POST-CIRCLE

Hold a dinner to celebrate and honour this Woman; create a joyous feast of celebration for her. And so it is.

GRANDMAMA BLESSING

A Circle to honour, celebrate and hold space for your grandmother or elder Women in your life

On their birthday/Mother's Day or a day sacred to them

*　　　*　　　*

There is a difference between getting older and becoming an elder. An elder is a Woman who has been initiated into her wisdom and who shares her teachings with the next generation.

How often I wish I could sit with my grandmothers and hear their tales, their struggles, their challenges and how they moved through them. How deeply I wish I had listened to their wisdom. For since they've both passed on, I find myself constantly seeking the wisdom of the elders in my life.

This Circle is an invitation to gather with the elders in your life, to give them the space to harvest, reflect and integrate the lessons they've learnt in their life, and to pass on any wisdom that you can bring forward into yours. This work is so sacred; it is ancient, it is what we've always done. This Circle is about reviving the reverence for the Women who came before us, the ones who have healed so much of our journeys, and who leave behind the keys to the work that we are being called to do.

WHO

The red thread (grandmothers, mother, daughters, great granddaughters)

GATHER

+ ritual basket (smudging tools, Oracle cards, matches, tea lights, candles, pen and paper for everyone)
+ 1 × plant pot
+ 1 × small bag of soil
+ 1 × big bunch of dried flowers
+ 1 × dried flower wreath (you can make or buy this beforehand)
+ 1 × pack of seed paper*

*Seed paper is a type of handmade paper that includes any number of different plant seeds

ALTAR

Fill the plant pot with soil and place it in the centre of the altar space. Create a flower circle using the dried flowers. Place tealights and candles in between the spaces. Place the dried flower wreath beside the space where your grandmama will sit. Keep the ritual basket close to the flower circle.

OPEN THE SPACE

Introduce yourself, the practice of the Women's Circle and the intention behind why you are gathering. Smudge the Women clockwise, then yourself, and then finally the altar space. Invite each Woman to introduce themselves and their astrology sign, and to share how they know the Elder.

ENERGY TALK

A grandmama blessing is a sacred space created to hold space and celebrate the elders in our lives, to listen to their stories, to soak in their wisdom, and to honour their life's journey.

MEDITATION

Invite the Circle to close their eyes, and gently begin to ground into the space, taking three deep inhalations, in through the nose and out through the mouth. Feel your bodies getting heavier and heavier as you ground into the earth beneath you.

SHARING PROMPTS

Invite the elder to begin to reflect on her life's journey, taking her back to when she was a fair maiden, and to any memories or moments in that time that jump out to her. What did she learn as a maiden? What lessons came through for her? How did she grow through her younger years?

Then invite her to journey to her mothering phase; how did it feel to become a mother? What did you learn? What moments jump out? What wisdom did you take from this fertile time in your life?

And finally, invite her to journey to her crone years, to the step she took over the threshold of menopause that has led her right here, to this very moment. What challenges did she face, what did she have to overcome? What wisdom does she sit on now?

As she takes this time to review her life, invite her to bring forward deep gratitude, honour and respect for the steps she has taken and the life she has so graciously and powerfully lived.

For we are gathering today to honour, celebrate and acknowledge the crown of the crone, the jewel in our lives who holds within her such deep pearls of wisdom for us.

As she opens her eyes, welcome her back into the space by placing the dried flower wreath on her head.

Invite the elder to share her life's journey. It is important to really hold the space and witness her in this moment, so if you have younger children present, please emphasise the importance of this.

Invite her to share anything that came up in her meditation, as she weaves through the journey of her life from Maiden to Mother to Crone.

+ What are the most powerful lessons she's learnt?
+ What does she want to pass onto you?
+ What does she ask that you take with you from her journey?

Once she's finished sharing, take a moment to honour her journey by going around and sharing what she brings to your life. How has the elder been there for you, supported you, taught you, cared for you?

Take this moment to honour all that she has done for you.

ORACLE CARDS

Invite the elder to receive the deck of cards and to shuffle them, asking to receive a message from the universe, to remind her of one last aspect of herself that she should honour. Encourage her to intuitively pull the card that calls to her, and then read the card to the Circle and invite anyone else to offer an interpretation to what it might be reflecting back.

RITUAL

This ritual is an act of honouring her life's journey as she sows her wisdom into the earth.

Taking the seeded paper from the ritual basket, invite her to tune into the deepest lessons she's learnt in this lifetime. As she writes them down, ask her to share them with you.

Then, stepping over to the altar space, invite her to plant the seeded paper into the plant pot using her hands, then seal over it with a jug of water, as she seeds her deepest lessons into the earth.

Pass the plant pot around to each Woman, with the invitation for them to tend to this plant, to water it, to nurture it, to remind them of the path she's paved for you through the obstacles, challenges, and experiences she has faced in her life.

Let this plant be a symbol of the seed that is sown, that flowers and then wilts, for such is the trifecta of Maiden, Mama, Crone.

POST-CIRCLE

Hold a dinner, tea party or lunch to feast, celebrate and honour the crown jewel in your life. Perhaps cook a family recipe, to symbolise the thread that connects you.

CLOSING WORDS

The intention behind this book was to create a manual that would serve you, your sisters, your daughters, your mothers, and all the Women in your community.

A book of inspiration that would begin to weave the threads of remembering back into your hands, so that you can go forth with confidence to create your own sacred spaces for you and the Women in your life to gather.

Remember, you do not need to be experienced in the Circle to do this work; I began all those years ago exactly where I was.

Start where you are and the medicine you hold will spread like magik. The more you hold space, the deeper your spaces will become.

My wish is that this book will water the seeds that live deep within you, the seeds your ancestors buried all those moons ago.

My wish is that one day soon, we will all look around and see flourishing gardens of sacred spaces blooming in every city, in every town, in every village, just as they once did; the Women's Circle restored back to our earth.

You hold it all in the palms of your hands. Let this book inspire you to remember.

It was always within you. For the truth of the Circle always remains: that it can never end.

ACKNOWLEDGEMENTS

This book is dedicated to my mother Sera, the infinite source of creativity, love and inspiration in my life. Your guidance led me to this path, and as you've passed the torch onto me, I know we are healing our feminine line together. This book is also dedicated to my daughter Luna. As I prepare to pass the torch onto you one day, my wish is that you carry it with all the light, strength, magik and courage of the women who came before you.

I wrote this book in honour of all the Women who came before me, and to all the ones to come after me. To the gifts, lessons, teachings and journeys we share.

The truth is, so many Women have helped me to bring this book to life.

You can't hold a Women's Circle by yourself, so how can you write a book on Women's Circles by yourself?

Thank you to all the Women who have contributed, supported, guided and held space for me as I birthed this book into being.

My teachers, my guides, my midwives.

Zoe Hind, thank you for taking me under your wing and helping me to remember.

Fiona Arrigo, for your elder wisdom and belief in me.

My doulas Samsara and Debbie, for holding space for me whilst birthing both my baby and this book.

Kathy Hertz, for being my Goddess Mama, and always being there to bring me back to me.

My book doula Saveira, thank you for creating the container for me to bring through this book.

Jane Hardwicke Collings, for your wisdom and the work you do.

To my sisters who supported this book in blooming.

Ste, the creatrix who joined on the wild ride and used her photographic gifts to capture the spirit and essence of the women's circle. I love you always.

Helena Doughty, for helping me weave the creation of this book together, and for being a constant supporter of love.

Nicci Harrison, for offering up your grief circle to this book. Thank you for sharing your deep medicine with us all. You can find Nicci @thegriefspace

Kumari, for looking after both me and Luna in this process and always. You will forever be my sister.

Carol Doughty, my mother in love, for always being there and supporting Luna and I.

Nicola, for seeing this book before it was here, and for believing in me, my words and my writing always.

To the book angels, who heard the calling that I needed support. I couldn't have dreamed of a more divine tribe of women who supported me in making this dream a reality.

Alice from Meadow Folk, thank you for your flowers, your seeds, all the flower circles you created and the magik you infused into them.

Alice from Home Farm Glamping, thank you for gifting us the privilege of using the most dreamy location to shoot our book.

Zoe from SouLand Yoga, thank you for welcoming us in to your sacred space, what a dream it was.

Alice, publisher at Hardie Grant, thank you for holding my vision and believing in me. Working with you has been a dream come true.

Tali Zeloof, for supporting and helping me to follow my art. Love you so much.

Valeria, my book agent, thank you for all your support and skills ensuring this book manifested.

To all the magikal women who gathered with me for the photoshoot, I still can't put into words what happened on that day; but know you all felt it. Honouring all of you: Camilla, Amelia, Gemma, Grace, Jess, Leonara, Nicci, Nina, Rebecca, Viviene, Kim, Farah, Paris, Melinda, Morgan, Minal. And to the little women who made my visions real: my sister Lyla, beautiful Pearl and Rachel, and of course my little star Luna.

Thank you to all the women doing this work already, and to all of you who are preparing to step back in.

And lastly, although I have hardly mentioned the Masculine in this book, the truth is I wouldn't be doing what I am doing without them. My husband, Michael, and my spirit dog, Harley, hold me in ways that the feminine can't. You are the guardians of my sacred space, the rocks in my life, my home. Thank you for all that you are.

PHOTOGRAPHY CREDITS

All photos were taken by Steph Marques apart from pages 4, 144 & 182, which were taken by Tali Photography.

207

Published in 2022 by Hardie Grant Books, an imprint of Hardie Grant Publishing

Hardie Grant Books (Melbourne)
Wurundjeri Country
Building 1, 658 Church Street
Richmond, Victoria 3121

Hardie Grant Books (London)
5th & 6th Floors
52–54 Southwark Street
London SE1 1UN

hardiegrantbooks.com

A catalogue record for this book is available from the National Library of Australia

The Women's Circle
ISBN 9781743797488
10 9 8 7 6 5 4 3 2 1

Commissioning Editor: Alice Hardie-Grant
Editor: Vanessa Lanaway
Design Manager: Kristin Thomas
Photographers: Steph Marques & Tali Photography
Production Manager: Todd Rechner
Production Coordinator: Jessica Harvie

Colour reproduction by Splitting Image Colour Studio
Printed in China by Leo Paper Products LTD.

MIX
Paper from responsible sources
FSC® C020056

Hardie Grant acknowledges the Traditional Owners of the country on which we work, the Wurundjeri people of the Kulin nation and the Gadigal people of the Eora nation, and recognises their continuing connection to the land, waters and culture. We pay our respects to their Elders past, present and emerging.